AQA Religious Studies A

Roman Catholicism: Ethics

GCSE

Robert Bowie

Series editor

Cynthia Bartlett

ornes

Published in 2009 by:
Nelson Thornes Ltd
Delta Place
27 Bath Road
CHELTENHAM
GL53 7TH
United Kingdom

11 12 13 / 10 9 8 7 6

A catalogue record for this book is available from the British Library

ISBN 978 1 4085 0510 6

Cover photograph by Will Howells
Illustrations by Paul McCaffrey (c/o Sylvie Poggio) and David Russell Illustration

Page make-up by Pantek Arts Ltd
Printed and bound in China by 1010 Printing International Ltd

The author and publisher are grateful to the following for permission to reproduce the following copyright material:

Photo acknowledgements

Alamy: 2.6B; 3.2A; 3.2C; 3.6A; 3.6B; 3.6C; 4.10C; 4.6B; 6.6C; 3.10B. ArkReligion.com/ Catholic Press Photo: 3.8C. Corbis: 1.7A. Fotolia: 1.1A; 1.2A; 1.3A; 1.3B; 1.3C; 1.5A; 1.5B; 1.6A; 1.6B; 2ExA; 2.4A; 2.4C; 2.4B; 2.7A; 2.8A; 2.8B; 3.2B; 3.4B; 3.5A; 3.5B; 3.8B; 3.9A; 3ExA; 4.1A; 4.2A; 4.3C; 4.8B; 4.9B; 4ExA; 5.1A; 5.10A; 5.2A; 5.3A; 5.3B; 5.4A; 5.4B; 5.4C; 5.5A; 5.6A; 5.6C; 5.7A; 5.8A;5.8B; 5.9A; 5ExA; 6.1A; 6.1B; 6.2A; 6.2B; 6.2C; 6.2D; 6.4B; 6.4C; 6.5A; 6.8A; 6.8B; 6.8C; 6.8D; 6.10A; 6.12A; 6.12B; 6ExA. Getty: 6.12C. Istockphoto: 1.5C; 2.2A; 2.7C; 3.7B; 6.3A; 6.9B. Rex: 1.7B; 4.7B; 4.10A; 4.11A; 6.7A; 6.7B; 6.11A; 6.11B.

Text acknowledgements

short extracts from *The Roman Catholic Catechism*, Burns and Oates. English translation for United Kingdom Copyright © 1974, 1999 Burns & Oates - Libreria Editrice Vaticana. Reprinted by permission of Continuum International Publishing Group UK; Scripture quotations taken from the Holy Bible, New International Version, Copyright © 1978, 1984 by International Bible Society. Used by permission of Hodder & Stoughton, a division of Hodder Headline Ltd. All rights reserved. "NIV" is a registered trademark of International Bible Society. UK trademark number 1448790; Canon Chris Chivers and Blackburn Cathedral, UK for the poem *Make Poverty History*; Deacon Mark Ripper and St. John's Church, Westminster MD for an extract from www. carr.org on the examination of priests; Ken Sewell and Liverpool Academic Press for an extract from *A Catholic Priest: Today and Tomorrow* by Michael Evans, 1993; Rob Casey and Saint John Houghton Catholic School for an extract from their school newsletter February 2008, by Rob Casey, 2008; St Edmunds Catholic Church for an extract from their online parish notices.

Thanks also to CAFOD (www.cafod.org.uk) and Trócaire (http://trocaire.org) for allowing us to reproduce their logos.

Every effort has been made to contact the copyright holders and we apologise if any have been overlooked. Should copyright have been unwittingly infringed in this book, the owners should contact the publishers, who will make corrections at reprint.

Contents

Nelson Thornes has worked in partnership with AQA to make sure that this book offers you the best possible support for your GCSE course. All the content has been approved by the senior examining team at AQA, so you can be sure that it gives you just what you need when you are preparing for your exams.

◼ How to use this book

This book covers everything you need for your course.

Learning Objectives

At the beginning of each section or topic you'll find a list of Learning Objectives based on the requirements of the specification, so you can make sure you are covering everything you need to know for the exam.

> **Objectives**
> **Objectives**
> **Objectives**
> **Objectives**
> First objective.
> Second objective.

AQA Examiner's Tips

Don't forget to look at the AQA Examiner's Tips throughout the book to help you with your study and prepare for your exam.

> **AQA Examiner's tip**
> Don't forget to look at the AQA Examiner's Tips throughout the book to help you with your study and prepare for your exam.

AQA Examination-style Questions

These offer opportunities to practise doing questions in the style that you can expect in your exam so that you can be fully prepared on the day.

AQA examination questions are reproduced by permission of the Assessment and Qualifications Alliance.

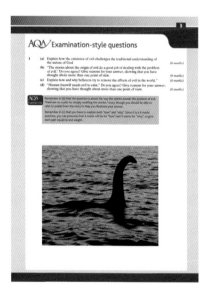

This book is written specifically for GCSE students studying the AQA Religious Studies Specification A, *Unit 4: Roman Catholicism: Ethics*. It looks at how Christians, and particularly Roman Catholic Christians, respond to moral questions, questions of right and wrong, good and bad.

You do not have to be religious or Roman Catholic to study this course. You simply need to be interested in ethical questions and what others think. You need to be willing to think deeply about your own opinions, and the beliefs and responses of Roman Catholic Christians. The unit will provide you with the opportunity to develop your knowledge, skills and understanding of ethics in the Roman Catholic tradition by exploring challenging moral questions. You will be asked to consider your own responses, as well as the responses of Roman Catholic Christians.

◼ Topics in this unit

In the examination you will be asked to answer questions taken from any of the topics. Topics may be mixed within questions. Chapters in this book are arranged around the topics in the unit:

Christian values

This topic examines how the key Biblical teachings, the Ten Commandments and the Beatitudes influence the attitudes of Christians today.

Christian marriage

This topic examines how Roman Catholic teaching informs Roman Catholic views on marriage, sexuality and family life. It will look at how these views influence attitudes towards the marriage rite, the idea of marriage, sexual relationships outside marriage, parenthood, adoption and fostering, marital breakdown, divorce remarriage and annulment.

Christian vocation

This topic considers different ways in which Roman Catholics can live out their vocation as ordained ministers, religious or lay people, and how views about serving God influences attitudes towards issues including the ordination of women, marriage for priests and celibacy.

The Sacrament of Reconciliation

This topic considers how and why Roman Catholic celebrate the Sacrament of Reconciliation and how these beliefs influences their attitudes to crime and punishment and prejudice and discrimination.

Christian healing

This topic considers Roman Catholic beliefs and attitudes related to the sick and dying and respect for human life in issues including contraception, abortion and euthanasia.

Christian responses to global issues

This topic looks at Roman Catholic beliefs, attitudes and responses to a number of global issues including world poverty and war and peace.

◼ Assessment guidance

The questions set in the examination will frequently require you to show a knowledge and understanding of Roman Catholic Christian beliefs and responses. The questions will sometimes be require you to give examples of different Christian responses, though these need not necessarily be opposing responses. Each chapter has an assessment guidance section at the end. It will help you to write better answers yourself, if you understand what the examiners are looking for when they mark these questions. To assist you in this, you will be asked to mark an example for yourself – using the mark scheme below. Make sure that you understand the differences between the standard of answer for each level, and what you need to do to achieve full marks.

Examination questions will test two assessment objectives:

AO1	Describe, explain and analyse, using knowledge and understanding.	50%
AO2	Use evidence and reasoned argument to express and evaluate personal responses, informed insights and differing viewpoints.	50%

Levels of response mark schemes

The examiner will also take into account the quality of your written communication – how clearly you express yourself and how well you communicate your meaning. The grid below also gives you some guidance on the sort of quality examiners expect to see at different levels.

Levels	Criteria for AO1	Criteria for AO2	Quality of written communication	Marks
0	Nothing relevant or worthy of credit	An unsupported opinion or no relevant evaluation	The candidate's presentation, spelling, punctuation and grammar seriously obstruct understanding	0 marks
Level 1	Something relevant or worthy of credit	An opinion supported by simple reason	The candidate presents some relevant information in a simple form. The text produced is usually legible. Spelling, punctuation and grammar allow meaning to be derived, although errors are sometimes obstructive	1 mark
Level 2	Elementary knowledge and understanding, e.g. two simple points	An opinion supported by one developed reason or two simple reasons		2 marks
Level 3	Sound knowledge and understanding	An opinion supported by one well developed reason or several simple reasons. N.B. Candidates who make no religious comment should not achieve more than Level 3	The candidate presents relevant information in a way which assists with the communication of meaning. The text produced is legible. Spelling, punctuation and grammar are sufficiently accurate not to obscure meaning	3 marks
Level 4	A clear knowledge and understanding with some development	An opinion supported by two developed reasons with reference to religion		4 marks
Level 5	A detailed answer with some analysis, as appropriate	Evidence of reasoned consideration of two different points of view, showing informed insights and knowledge and understanding of religion	The candidate presents relevant information coherently, employing structure and style to render meaning clear. The text produced is legible. Spelling, punctuation and grammar are sufficiently accurate to render meaning clear	5 marks
Level 6	A full and coherent answer showing good analysis, as appropriate	A well-argued response, with evidence of reasoned consideration of two different points of view showing informed insights and ability to apply knowledge and understanding of religion effectively		6 marks

Note: In evaluation answers to questions worth only 3 marks, the first three levels apply. Questions which are marked out of 3 marks do not ask for two views, but reasons for your own opinion.

Successful study of this unit will result in a Short Course GCSE award. Study of one further unit will provide a Full Course GCSE award. Other units in Specification A which may be taken to achieve a Full Course GCSE award are:

- Unit 1 Christianity
- Unit 2 Christianity: Ethics
- Unit 3 Roman Catholicism
- Unit 5 St Mark's Gospel
- Unit 6 St Luke's Gospel
- Unit 7 Philosophy of Religion
- Unit 8 Islam
- Unit 9 Islam: Ethics
- Unit 10 Judaism
- Unit 11 Judaism: Ethics
- Unit 12 Buddhism
- Unit 13 Hinduism
- Unit 14 Sikhism

1.1 Making moral decisions

Making moral decisions

How we choose to live, what we choose to do or not do, reflects our values, principles, attitudes and beliefs. The choices that we make matter to us, but Christians believe they matter to God as well. Making moral decision is not simply about how we deal with particular issues in life, but how we live.

Discussion activity

1 When people make moral decisions, what do you think affects their choices?
   a Their desires/wishes?
   b Their beliefs?
   c Their will power?
   d Their intelligence?
   e Peer pressure?
   f Their upbringing?

Christian living can be seen in different ways. It is following God's laws, treating people with love and respect, trying to act in a virtuous (moral) way, listening to **conscience**, the voice of God inside.

When trying to decide how a Christian might act, these are the guiding principles that motivate Christian behaviour. These principles and values are based on the Ten Commandments and teachings of Jesus as shown in the beatitudes.

Human dignity and human rights

The Bible says that all human beings are made in the image and likeness of God (see Genesis 1:26). Human beings have **dignity** and human life is sacred. Christians cannot simply treat people as objects, as tools to be used for some greater purpose because all human beings have a greater purpose, as creations of God.

Activities

1 Suggest 3 different ways in which a person could treat another with dignity, compassion and respect.
2 Describe an example of when you or someone close to you felt you were not treated with dignity, or when you felt you were treated with dignity.
3 What do you think it means to have dignity, or be treated with dignity? Give examples to explain your answer.

Objectives

Identify and interpret ideas of dignity, happiness, conscience, freedom and responsibility, and apply them to situations as Christians might do.

Key terms

Conscience: a person's sense of right and wrong. For many Christians it is linked to God.

Dignity: the value of a human person.

Sin: behaviour which is against God's laws and wishes/against the principles of morality. A thought or action which is wrong, we know is wrong and we freely choose.

AQA Examiner's tip

The topics covered on these pages are not specifically examined but they will help you understand how a Roman Catholic Christian makes moral decisions.

links

For more information on the Ten Commandments, see pages 12 to 17. For more information on the Beatitudes, see pages 18 to 21.

AQA Examiner's tip

Belief in human dignity and human rights is especially important to remember when you are answering questions on abortion and euthanasia; this links to the commandment not to commit murder.

Conscience and freedom

The Catholic Church teaches that conscience is a powerful voice or law, deep within a person which connects God's moral truth with our instincts, feelings and thoughts. It helps people to do good and avoid evil. We must not ignore our conscience and should act in accordance with it. Conscience needs to be informed or trained through studying the teachings of the Church and also through prayer.

A   *Conscience should be informed by prayer and study of the Church's teachings*

■ Responsibility and sin

The Roman Catholic Church teaches that human beings were made to be free, but they should act in the service of love, not selfishness or evil. Great responsibility comes with the freedom that God has given humans.

Human sin can lead conscience astray. Humans have a natural weakness called Original Sin. This is a tendency towards **sin** inherited from the sin of Adam and Eve. However, God's law, found in the Church's teachings, is an important guide which helps human conscience overcome sin.

■ The Catechism of the Catholic Church

A number of sources are used in this book but there are frequent references to the Catechism of the Catholic Church, an authoritative summary of Roman Catholic teaching.

Summary

You should now understand that Christians try to live according to important principles.

1.2   Virtues, gifts and fruits of the Spirit

■ The virtues and the gifts and fruits of the Spirit

In Catholic teaching, virtue is the power of doing good. Human beings have the capacity for that power within themselves but it must be encouraged and trained and the Holy Spirit helps people to do this.

Beliefs and teachings

St Paul said:

> Finally, brothers, whatever is true, whatever is noble, whatever is right, whatever is pure, whatever is lovely, whatever is admirable – if anything is excellent or praiseworthy – think about such things.
>
> *Philippians* 4:8

> Put on the full armour of God so that you can take your stand against the devil's schemes.
>
> *Ephesians* 6:10

Virtue then is like a habit, a way of living out the beliefs, values and moral teachings in life. It requires practice and the help of God through gifts from Holy Spirit. A Christian will show signs of this help in the fruits of the spirit; that is, in the way he or she will behave towards others.

Beliefs and teachings

> The aim of the virtuous life is to become like God.
>
> *Catechism* 1804

Cardinal virtues

Cardinal virtues are sometimes referred to as human or moral virtues as they can be discovered through human reason. These are:

- 'prudence': the commonsense or practical wisdom to make the right decision and see it through
- 'justice': the sense of fair play towards God and neighbour
- 'power' or 'fortitude': the courage and strength to get through difficulties which are faced in moral decision-making
- 'temperance': living life in moderation, rather than to excess.

Theological virtues

These come from St Paul's teachings and connect human beings with God. These are:

- 'faith': which enables Christians to believe in God and his teachings
- 'hope': encourages Christians to trust in God's promise to humankind
- 'love': (sometimes called 'charity') is the very basis of the Christian life encompassing the love of God, the love of neighbour and the love of self.

Objectives

Identify and interpret the virtues and gifts of the Spirit, and apply them to situations as Christians might do.

Key terms

Gifts of the Holy Spirit: qualities from the Holy Spirit which will help a Christian to live a holy life.

Fruits of the Holy Spirit: signs of the Holy Spirit in Christian behaviour.

AQA   Examiner's tip

These pages are not examined but they will help you understand how a Roman Catholic Christian makes moral decisions.

Activity

1   Using newspapers or online news sources identify a series of actions of people in the stories which either demonstrate these virtues or show lack of them.

A

The gifts and fruits of the Spirit

The virtues are completed by the gifts of the Spirit received at baptism. The seven **gifts of the Holy Spirit** are 'wisdom, understanding, counsel, fortitude, knowledge, piety (worshipping God) and respect or fear of the Lord' (Catechism 1831).

Beliefs and teachings

May your good Spirit lead me on level ground?

Psalms 143:10

because those who are led by the Spirit of God are sons of God

Romans 8:14

The twelve **fruits of the Holy Spirit** also received in baptism are the signs of perfection in Christian living. Traditionally they are listed as: charity, joy, peace, patience, kindness, goodness, generosity, gentleness, faithfulness, modesty, self-control, chastity.

For Christians these virtues, gifts and fruits can all be found in the teachings of the Bible, especially in the commandments and the Beatitudes.

Activities

2   Look through this book and choose three topic areas at random. How might a Christian show one or more of the fruits of the spirit in what they choose to do in that example?

3   How easy was it to connect the ideas of the fruits of the Spirit with the topics? If it was not straightforward or easy, why do you think that was? In one of the situations where it was difficult to connect the topic with the ideas of the fruits of the spirit, what might a Christian do to help them make the link?

Extension activity

Consider some well-known people or friends or family you look up to. What virtues do you think they show? What virtue do you think is most important?

AQA   **Examiner's tip**

When you think about how a Christian may respond to a moral issue, think of the commandments and the Beatitudes and also the virtues that they inspire. For instance, all of them are linked to love in some way and righteousness is linked to justice.

Summary

You should now understand that Christians try to live by adopting the virtues and showing the fruits of the Spirit in their daily lives.

What are the Ten Commandments?

What are the Ten Commandments?

The Bible records that the Ten **Commandments** were revealed to Moses on Mount Sinai. They are believed by Christians to be the word of God and were seen to be part of the Covenant, or agreement, between God and man. In following the commandments people identify themselves as God's people. The Church teaches that the Ten Commandments show the duties that a Christian has, both to God and to neighbour.

Misconceptions and interpretations

When studying the Ten Commandments there are some common misconceptions and different interpretations:

- Some believe that there is only one version. In fact there are two versions (Exodus 20 and Deuteronomy 5) and they are not exactly the same (this book follows the Catechism in defining the commandments).
- The phrase 'the Ten Commandments' is not found anywhere in the Bible although many Christians use that phrase. In fact the translation 'ten sayings' or 'ten words' is more accurate.
- Some see the commandments, and Christian living, as living by a set of regulations. However, this does not reflect the beauty of the freedom God has given all human beings.
- Some argue that Christians are not bound by any rules, but this does not reflect that idea that that the commandments help people to live a happy and fulfilling life.

A better way of understanding the commandments

Another way of understanding the commandments is to see them as a gift of freedom, freedom from the slavery of sin and offering a way of living which helps Christians become more fully human. The Church calls them the 'path of life' (Catechism 2057).

Beliefs and teachings

I run along the way of your commandments, for you have set my heart free.

Psalms 119:32

Why do Christians try to follow the commandments?

In Christian life the commandments have a central role. They are often found on the walls of churches and cathedrals. When a young man asked Jesus, 'Teacher, what good must I do to get eternal life?' Jesus replied, 'If you wish to enter into life, keep the commandments,' and he then said, 'come follow me' (Matthew 19:16–17).

Objectives

Explore the Ten Commandments and the different ways in which they are understood and applied to Christian living.

Examine the Roman Catholic Church's teaching on the commandments.

Key terms

Commandment: a rule for living, given by God; or one of the Ten Commandments.

Extension activity

1. Look up Exodus 20 and Deuteronomy 5 and compare the different accounts. Can you spot any differences?
2. Consider what a society would be like without rules. In what sense would human beings be free?

Thinking about the commandments

As I came downstairs on Christmas morning one year, I saw a large, unwrapped present standing beside the tree. I stared in disbelief at a tag that bore my name. A beautiful, shiny, new bicycle.

I had to learn to ride first. My father held the back of my bike to steady me as a wobbled along. Every so often he would let go for a moment, to see whether I could manage alone. He gave me plenty of advice: 'Look straight ahead, don't look down. Don't be afraid, I've got hold of you. Push your feet downwards, left, right, left, right, use your toes.' The more I practised, the more confident I became, and soon I was whizzing up and down the streets, obeying my father's advice without even needing to think about it.

At first I was only allowed to cycle as far as the lamp-post.

Soon I was allowed to visit my friends if my older sister went with me, and eventually I was allowed on the road on my own. Then I was taught more rules – important rules that would protect me on the road. I was taught to use my arms to signal which way I wanted to turn, and to look behind me to see whether any cars were coming before moving into the middle of the road to make a right turn.

I used that wonderful present for years and learned many things that helped me to become more independent and wiser. However, the present my parents gave me could have been a deadly weapon if I hadn't followed the rules properly. Depending on whether I obeyed the rules of the road, the commandments, my present could lead to great joy, or terrible family grief.

(based upon an extract by John Redford from *Faith Alive* (1944)

A   *Following the road*

B   *A hard path to follow*

C   *Journey through the maze*

Activities

1   Draw two pictures, one that shows how the commandments may be reflected as regulations, and one that shows how they may be thought to be liberating. For example you could see the commandments as pointing the way to a better life, or as rules which must not be broken.

2   What do Photos **A**, **B** and **C** suggest about the commandments?

∞ links

To see the text of the Ten Commandments, turn over to page 14.

AQA   *Examiner's tip*

Make sure you can say more about what the commandments are, apart from simply being a list of rules.

Summary

You should now know that the Ten Commandments are understood by some to be rules and that the Catholic Church teaches that they are liberating laws which can free people from the slavery of sin.

The Ten Commandments: loving God

▪ The Law of Love underpins the Ten Commandments

The Church teaches that Jesus interpreted the Ten Commandments in the light of the Law of Love. This is a kind of love which expects nothing in return and shows a commitment to others. Each of the commandments expresses love in some way. Jesus summarised the Ten Commandments as loving God and loving your neighbour but 'love your neighbour' is not actually listed in the Ten Commandments.

A *The Ten Commandments*

Commandment	Summary in the Law of Love
1 I am the Lord your God, you shall not have other gods before me	Loving God
2 You shall not take the name of the Lord your God in vain	
3 Remember the Sabbath, to keep it holy	
4 Honour your father and mother	Loving your neighbour
5 You shall not kill	
6 You shall not commit adultery	
7 You shall not steal	
8 You shall not bear false witness against your neighbour	
9 You shall not covet your neighbour's wife	
10 You shall not covet your neighbour's possessions	

Objectives

Explore how the Law of Love underpins the commandments.

Examine how the commandments show a love of God and apply them to Christian living today.

Beliefs and teachings

love the Lord your God, with all your heart, and with all your soul, and with all your mind … love your neighbour as yourself. All the law and the prophets hang on these two commandments.

Matthew 22:37

∞ links

These pages cover the commandments about loving God. For more about the commandments about loving your neighbour, see pages 16–17.

▪ Loving God

1 I am the Lord your God, you shall not have other gods before me

The first commandment can be understood in different ways:

- God saved his people from the bondage of Egyptian slavery so he alone should be worshipped rather than the other gods worshipped at that time.

- In the modern world there are other things which people worship or follow as if they were gods, including superstition and magic, money, power or sex. Following these false gods will not lead to ultimate happiness and satisfaction. Jesus said, 'No servant can serve two masters' (Luke 16:13).

- Images must not be worshipped, although images and statues of Mary, Jesus or the Saints can be used to venerate the person who is shown.

- Christians are free to seek out the truth but once they have found it they are morally obliged to follow it and not choose other things or gods to worship instead.

B *False God?*

2 You shall not take the name of the Lord your God in vain

Respect for God's name is shown by blessing and praising it:

- Using God's name in blasphemy or curses is wrong. Jesus said, 'Do not swear at all' (Matthew 5:34).
- Promises made in the name of God or as a religious vow (for example during a wedding ceremony) should be kept, otherwise it will have been used trivially.

3 Remember the Sabbath, to keep it holy

For Christians the Sabbath is a holy day to be kept special and for worshipping God:

- Jesus understood the value of the Sabbath for human beings: 'The sabbath was made for man, not man for the sabbath' (Mark 2:27).
- Christians remember Sunday as the day of Christ's Resurrection. It is called the Day of the Lord.
- Sunday is kept holy by celebrating Mass, giving time for worship, prayer, the word (Bible) and Holy Communion.
- It is a time for family life and health, for caring for family and friends, enjoying rest and leisure and caring for the sick and elderly.

∞ links

For more on the marriage vows see pages 28 and 29. For religious vows see pages 58 and 59.

AQA Examiner's tip

Each commandment can be applied in many different ways. Make sure that you are able to give at least two different examples for each one.

Activities

1 Copy and complete the table below.

Commandment	Have no other Gods before me	You shall not take the Lord's name in vain	Remember the Sabbath, to keep it holy
Which virtue or virtues are encouraged?	Faithfulness to the true God		
What is prohibited?	Superstition, magic, money, power, sex		
What harm can be done by breaking the command and to whom?	Trusting in something which is not God will not lead to satisfaction, only frustration		

2 What things in the modern world might people be in danger of worshipping? Working in pairs, each person thinks of something which arguably might be worshipped (which is not God). Exchange these ideas with another pair.

3 You now have to build a case for why a Christian would argue that the thing your neighbour gave you should not be worshipped?

4 On what occasions might a Christian bless or praise God's name?

5 How might a Christian who has to work on Sunday due to their profession (for instance a nurse, doctor or fire-fighter) be able to show they remember the Sabbath? Would they have to change their job or is there another way they can obey this commandment? Consider both suggestions and any others you can think of and write down the most convincing answer.

Summary

You should now understand that the Ten Commandments are based on the Law of Love and that the first three commandments explore how Christians show a love of God.

4 Honour your father and mother

Parents should be honoured and respected as they have the responsibility of educating children in faith and life:

- Children owe respect, gratitude and obedience to their parents to support family life.
- Adult sons and daughters should care for their parents and provide support in times of illness, loneliness or old age.

5 You shall not kill

Christians must respect human life:

- Killing threatens peace and Christians are called to be peacemakers (Matthew 5:9).
- The commandment forbids murder, abortion, euthanasia and suicide.
- It is legitimate to defend life, even sometimes if that involves killing the attacker.
- Execution by the state of a criminal should not be necessary except in cases where there is a grave threat to the life of others that cannot be prevented through imprisonment.

6 You shall not commit adultery

Adultery is an example of unchastity:

- Chastity is a moral virtue. It involves being in control of human freedom and acting modestly and considerately. It requires prayer and self-knowledge.
- Adultery itself involves cheating on someone and breaks the marriage vows.

A *Why honour parents?*

B *Adultery*

Objectives

Explore how love of neighbour is expressed through the Ten Commandments.

Consider examples of different ways in which Christians apply the Ten Commandments.

Key terms

Adultery: sex outside marriage where one or both of the couple are already married to someone else.

Bear false witness: to lie.

Covet: wish, long, or crave for something, especially the property of another person or someone.

⚭links

See the Glossary at the back of this book for definitions of terms that you are unsure about.

Activity

1 How do adultery, pornography, prostitution and rape undermine the dignity of the human person (refer back to pages 8 to 9 if necessary)?

- The Church teaches that this commandment forbids all sins against chastity including pornography, prostitution and rape which all undermine the dignity of the human person.
- Jesus said, 'Anyone who looks at a woman lustfully, he has already committed adultery with her in his heart.' (Matthew 5:28) and also 'The spirit is willing, but the body is weak.' (Matthew 26:41).

7 You shall not steal

Stealing, taking property which is not yours, is wrong. Stealing shows a lack of respect for the work and effort of others:

- Christians must respect both the fair distribution of the world's wealth and the ownership of private property.
- Theft is forbidden and this includes paying unjust wages, forgery, corruption, damaging things held in common, such as public facilities.
- Christians must not force people to work in harsh or undignified conditions, or for unjust wages.

8 You shall not bear false witness against your neighbour

- Christians are called to live truthfully.
- Truthfulness is part of public and private living. It affects work, community, friends and family.
- The commandment forbids **bearing false witness**, perjury and lying (which distort truth) as well as slander, defamation and malicious speech (which undermine reputations).
- A crime against truth harms people as it undermines trust, friendship and the community.

9 You shall not covet your neighbour's wife

- Christians must overcome sexual thoughts and desires linked to the sixth commandment (you shall not commit adultery).
- Such thoughts may lead to that commandment being broken, and may show a lack of respect for others and disloyalty.
- Christians must seek a pure heart and modesty to protect and respect each human person's dignity.

10 You shall not covet your neighbour's possessions

- Christians must respect the property of others.
- Greed, envy and unbridled **covetousness** must all be avoided. This means it is wrong to live life only for the things that can be bought, and wrong to try and get as much as is possible for yourself.
- Covetousness makes a person self-centred and selfish, and is against the Law of Love. Jesus praises the 'poor in spirit' (Matthew 5:3), encouraging his followers not to become attached to possessions.

Activities

2   What is being stolen when unjust wages are paid?

3   Who has been robbed when public buildings are damaged or destroyed?

C   Theft

Activities

4   Look back to the table in Activity 1 on page 15 and draw one like it showing the remaining commandments.

5   What do you think might be meant by the phrase 'living in truth'?

6   How might crimes against truth harm people?

7   'Surely there is nothing wrong with bad thoughts – after all they harm no-one!' Who might bad thoughts harm? Can you think of examples where thoughts become dangerous?

8   What is the difference between greed and trying to provide a good living for yourself and family?

Summary

You should now understand that the Ten Commandments reflect the law to love your neighbour and that the Roman Catholic Church teaches that each of the commandments can be applied in different ways to many aspects of Christian Life.

AQA   Examiner's tip

Make sure you can show how each of the seven commandments referred to here are related to loving your neighbour.

Introduction to the Beatitudes

Jesus taught the **Beatitudes** as part of his **Sermon on the Mount**.

The Beatitudes use the phrase 'blessed are' which is sometimes translated as 'how happy are'. This phrase does not mean blessing in the usual sense; for example, it would be very strange to say that poor starving people are happy and have blessings. These people are blessed because they are close to God and the **Kingdom of God** is for them.

The Beatitudes point to the goal of all human action, being close to God.

Beliefs and teachings

Blessed are the poor in spirit, for theirs is the kingdom of heaven.

Blessed are those who mourn, for they will be comforted.

Blessed are the meek, for they will inherit the earth.

Blessed are those who hunger and thirst for righteousness, for they will be filled.

Blessed are the merciful, for they will be shown mercy.

Blessed are the pure in heart, for they will see God.

Blessed are the peacemakers, for they will be called children of God.

Blessed are those who are persecuted because of righteousness, for theirs is the kingdom of heaven.

Blessed are you when people insult you, persecute you and falsely say all kinds of evil against you because of me. Rejoice and be glad, because great is your reward in heaven, for in the same way they persecuted the prophets who were before you.

Matthew 5:3-12

The Beatitudes are a route to eternal happiness

The Church teaches that human beings were created to seek happiness and the greatest happiness, above all things, is happiness with God, the ultimate Beatitude.

Jesus' teachings in the Beatitudes point the way for followers of Christ to eternal happiness. They may be difficult to follow, so Christians need God's help to live life according to the Beatitudes. God calls all people to happiness with him and he provides people with the ultimate satisfaction.

The Beatitudes in detail

Blessed are the poor in spirit, for theirs is the kingdom of heaven (Matthew 5:3)

Poverty is real and is not seen as a good thing in the Old Testament (see Deuteuronomy 15:11). Jesus came to bring about the Kingdom of God; he announced freedom for the downtrodden and spent his life with outcasts and the poor rather than with the rich.

Objectives

Explore the meaning of the beatitudes and suggest different ways in which they are understood and applied by Christians.

Key terms

Beatitude: meaning 'blessed' or 'happy'. The Beatitudes is the beginning portion of the Sermon on the Mount. In it, Jesus describes the qualities of the inhabitants of the Kingdom of heaven and indicates how each is or will be blessed.

Sermon on the Mount: a collection of Jesus Christ's religious and moral teachings recorded in Matthew's Gospel in the Bible, much of which Jesus Christ set out in a speech to his disciples from a hillside.

Kingdom of God: wherever God is honoured as king and his authority accepted. Jesus taught about the Kingdom of God both on earth and in heaven. The rule of God.

Beliefs and teachings

We all want to live happily.
St Augustine

God alone satisfies.
St Thomas Aquinas

Catechism 1718

Activity

1. Think of three different meanings of the word 'happiness'. How are they different from or similar to the kind of happiness described on this page?

Being poor in spirit suggest an attitude of mind, an approach to life based on humility and morality, rather than one of excess and self-centredness. God is close to the poor because they understand a need for him. Living a Christian life means living a simple life and being detached from wealth.

Blessed are the meek, for they will inherit the earth (Matthew 5:4)

This Beatitude refers to those who are humble and gentle and do not put themselves before others: in other words they put themselves last and God and others first.

Jesus gave himself in the service of others. People who are meek put the concerns of others before their own, they recognise the dignity of the human person and they are rewarded.

Blessed are those who mourn, for they will be comforted (Matthew 5:5)

There are many evils in the world, many wrongs being done and those who are good mourn because of these evils and wish for God's will to be done instead. This Beatitude shows the sense of suffering, not for their own loss, but for the loss in the world. God brings these people the comfort of his kingdom.

A   *Those who choose the life of a monk or nun, or choose to be a member of a religious order, take a vow of poverty*

Activities

2   What is the difference between physical poverty and spirtitual poverty?

3   How may other Christians live a life that is poor in spirit, and why might physical poverty not be enough?

B   *A statue by Josefina de Vasconcellos. It was given to Coventry Cathedral on the 50th anniversary of the end of World War II (1995). A replica of this statue was donated by the people of Coventry to the peace garden of Hiroshima in Japan. During World War II Coventry was bombed by Germany and Hiroshima was bombed by America*

AQA   Examiner's tip

Remember that there are different ways in which people can be poor.

Activity

4   Which Beatitudes are demonstrated by this statue, and the people of Coventry? Explain your answer.

Summary

You should now understand that Christians seek happiness for others and happiness in God and that the Beatitudes help them work out how to achieve this.

Blessed are those who hunger and thirst for righteousness, for they will be filled (Matthew 5:6)

This means having a desire for religious and moral perfection (**righteousness**).To seek righteousness includes hungering after God's justice throughout the world. True happiness and satisfaction can only be found in God.

> 66 *The struggle against injustice and the pursuit of truth cannot be separated nor can one work for one independent of the other.* 99
>
> Ignatio Ellacuría, S.J. (Superior of Jesuit community who was assassinated, along with five others, a housekeeper and her daughter, because of the community's work for justice)

Blessed are the merciful, for they will be shown mercy (Matthew 5:7)

In the Bible it is traditionally God who shows **mercy**, God who forgives, and God who does not give up on people, so being merciful is being God-like. Showing mercy is showing love and forgiveness (Matthew 6:12, 14:15, 18:35).

In the Lord's Prayer (Matthew 6:9–13 and Luke 11:1–4), Christians ask for forgiveness as they have forgiven others.

Showing mercy is a big step – Jesus forgives when he is crucified on the cross even though people do not ask for forgiveness.

Blessed are the pure in heart for they will see God (Matthew 5:8)

Purity of heart is the attitude of being committed and dedicated to God. Thoughtless outward signs are not good enough. A person who is pure in heart is just and fair in their dealings with others.

For some people purity is all about keeping clean, which includes not eating the wrong food, but Jesus said people are not made unclean by what goes into the mouth but rather what comes out. Being impure inside can lead to the breaking of the commandments such as murder, adultery and many other evils (see Matthew 15:10, 17–20). For Christians to become pure-hearted, they must first recognise their own shortcomings and impurity, and pray for God's help (see Psalms 51 and Luke 18:8–15).

Blessed are the peacemakers, for they will be called children of God (Matthew 5:9)

The Hebrew word for **peace** is Shalom and can it be translated as well-being, prosperity, happiness and fulfilment. Peace means much more than the lack of war, but the reconciliation of all divided people.

Christians are sent by God to bring the people divided by conflict back together. This is what it means to be a child of God. Jesus taught that

---

Objectives

Examine different ways in which the beatitudes are understood by Christians and how they may be applied in Christian life.

Interpret the actions of some Christians in terms of the beatitudes.

Key terms

Righteousness: following moral principles.

Mercy: to be kind and forgiving.

Peace: an absence of war and conflict.

Activities

1. Why is it so hard to forgive? Think of an example where it might be very difficult to forgive and try to identify the thoughts and feelings which make forgiveness difficult.

2. Why might Christians say that forgiveness that is difficult is especially important?

Activity

3. What do you think is meant by the phrase a pure heart or an impure heart? Suggest how the purity of someone's heart might affect what they do.

AQA Examiner's tip

Remember that peace is not just the absence of war.

to be at peace with God, people must be at peace with their brothers, sisters, all Christians and others in the community (Matthew 5:23–24). Jesus reconciled everyone to God on the cross and so he is the ultimate peacemaker (John 12:23).

Blessed are those who are persecuted because of righteousness, for theirs is the kingdom of heaven (Matthew 5:10)
Blessed are you when people insult you, persecute you and falsely say all kinds of evil against you because of me. Rejoice and be glad, because great is your reward in heaven, for in the same way they persecuted the prophets who were before you. (Matthew 5:11–12)

Followers of Jesus may be persecuted, reviled and suffer false accusation, mockery and other hardships.

Those who are persecuted because of their faith are given a share in the Kingdom of God. The path to holiness is hard but the reward is eternal happiness with God.

Jesus is the highest example of this with his suffering in Gethsemane and throughout the Passion, ultimately accepting crucifixion. The prophets, who were concerned for justice, were also persecuted.

Activities

4   Why might some Christians interpret this as a call for all Christians to embrace pacifism (non violence)?

5   How could it be argued this is not the case?

Activity

6   Look at the case studies below. Which of the Beatitudes did Fr Maximilian Kolbe and Oscar Romeo demonstrate in their lives?

St Maximilian Mary Kolbe

Fr Maximilian Mary Kolbe was a priest who led missions to Japan, founding a monastery in Nagasaki. During the war he provided shelter for Jews fleeing persecution in Poland. He was arrested and sent to the Auschwitz concentration camp. While in the camp some men were chosen to be starved to death because one had escaped. Fr Kolbe volunteered to take the place of a man who was lamenting his family. He led the men in prayer and hymns until, he, the last survivor, was given a lethal injection. He was canonised a saint in 1982 and declared a martyr.

A

Case study

Oscar Romero

Oscar Romero was Archbishop of San Salvador in El Salvador. He witnessed violations of human rights, murders, disappearances and torture, carried out by the government. Many suffered terribly at this time and Romero denounced the actions of the government forces. During his Masses he spoke out against the persecution, reading lists of 'disappeared' people. In 1980, as he was holding up the consecrated host at mass in his Cathedral, he was shot dead by a member of a right-wing group.

B

Case study

Summary

You should now be able to explain some of the ways in which Christians might apply the Beatitudes in their lives.

1

Christian values – summary

For the examination you should now be able to:

✔ explain the terms commandment and Beatitude

✔ explain the way the Ten Commandments might be viewed as rules or a guide for life

✔ explain how the commandments are related to loving God and loving each other

✔ explain the way the Beatitudes can be seen as ways of bringing happiness to others and finding happiness in God

✔ outline how Christians interpret the commandments and the Beatitudes, using examples of Christians who have lived lives by them.

Sample answer

1 Write an answer to the following exam question.

Explain how Christians might respond to the Beatitude, 'Blessed are the pure of heart, for they will see God'.

(3 marks)

2 Read the following sample answer:

> Christians believe that a person's inner attitude really matters to God. Being pure means being honest and fair. A dishonest or unfair person will probably end up breaking the commandments such as 'Do not commit adultery'.

3 With a partner, discuss the sample answer. Do you think that there are other things that the student could have included in the answer?

4 What mark would you give this answer out of 3? Look at the mark scheme in the Introduction on page 7 (AO1). What are the reasons for the mark you have given?

∞ links

Practice exam questions on how Christian values are applied to specific areas are found in later assessment guidance sections.

AQA Examination-style questions

1 Look at the illustrations and answer the following questions.

A *The Ten Commandments*

B *The Beatitudes*

(a) Give two of the Ten Commandments which refer to loving God. *(2 marks)*

(b) Explain how Christians may respond to these commandments in the way they live their lives. *(4 marks)*

  Remember you need to make direct links between the commandments and the actions or choices a Christian makes.

(c) 'Blessed are those who are persecuted because of righteousness'. Explain briefly this Beatitude and suggest how it might help Christians facing persecution. *(3 marks)*

(d) 'The Ten Commandments are not very helpful to life in the modern world'. Do you agree? Give reasons for your answer showing that you have thought about more than one point of view. *(6 marks)*

  Remember when you are asked if you agree with a statement, you must show what you think and the reasons why other people might not agree with you. If your answer is one-sided you will only achieve a maximum of 4 marks. If you make no religious comment then you will achieve no more than 3 marks.

2.1 Introduction to marriage in society

Case study

Thought-provoking statements on marriage

" *Marriage is three parts love and seven parts forgiveness of sins.* "
Lao Tzu, Chinese Taoist philosopher 600–531 BCE

" *For two people in a marriage to live together day after day is unquestionably the one miracle the Vatican has overlooked.* "
Bill Cosby, American actor/entertainer

" *Marriage is not a noun; it's a verb. It isn't something you get. It's something you do. It's the way you love your partner every day.* "
Barbara De Angelis, relationship expert

" *The goal in marriage is not to think alike, but to think together.* "
Robert C. Dodds, psychologist and marriage counsellor

" *More marriages might survive if the partners realised that sometimes the better comes after the worse.* "
Doug Larson, English middle-distance runner, 1902–1981, who won gold medals at the 1924 Olympic Games in Paris

Objectives

Know how different people have understood the idea of marriage.

Be able to discuss different views of marriage including your own and give reasons for them.

Activities

1 In the Case Study what is each person trying to say about marriage?

2 Do you agree? Give reasons for your views.

Are people giving up on marriage?

Research suggests that couples in Britain are getting married later and later, on average after they have turned 30. Many people live together before getting married. In 2004 the UK passed a law which permitted same sex couples to have what is called a civil partnership legally recognised. Some Christians believe these changes are threatening Christian **marriage**.

Some statistics on marriage

- In 2006 there were 236,980 weddings in England and Wales, the lowest number for almost a hundred years.
- Of these, 144,120 were first marriages for both parties (61 per cent)
- The average age for first marriages in England and Wales is 31 for men and 29 for women.

Provisional statistics from the office of National Statistics www.statistics.gov.uk

On the other hand!

Research suggests that not everyone has given up on marriage:

- Researchers asked people what they thought getting married means. The most popular answer was 'committing yourself to being faithful to your partner'.
- 85 per cent of people getting married say they intend to remain faithful.

Key terms

Marriage: a legal union between a man and a woman. The sacramental union between a man and a woman in the Roman Catholic Church witnessed by a priest and the community.

∞ links

For a definition of Christian marriage, please see page 26.

Mr and Mrs Lewis of Margam, Near Port Talbot celebrated their 70th (Platinum) anniversary in 2008. They were married in July 1938, and have spent their lives together. They were only parted when Mr Lewis served in the RAF during World War II for 6 years.

- Over 60 per cent of the population see extramarital sex as always wrong.
- Divorce rates in the UK have fallen to the lowest number since 1985. In 2006 only 12 people in every thousand who were married got divorced (though this still meant 148,141 divorces in 2006).

A very brief history of marriage

Marriage has changed enormously over the last century. Roman Catholic psychologist Dr Jack Dominion wrote that before modern times, marriage was based far more on economic and social necessity. People were probably much more willing to put up with an unhappy situation, because they could not afford to live separately.

The idea that marriage is based on a loving and equal relationship is a fairly new development. If people want to split up, they can do so financially because women are able to work now.

Yes, I will marry the middle one.

A *Equality and love are essential ingredients in Christian marriage. Times have changed*

Legal and religious ideas of marriage

Some suggest there is a lot of confusion between the legal idea of marriage and the specifically Christian vision of marriage. Christian marriage is a commitment to the other person and to God.

In many countries the kind of marriage which is recognised by law is based on the religious tradition of that country. So civil marriages in the UK are based on the Christian idea of marriage, but there are some important differences:

- A wedding in Church might be recognised by the Church but is not recognised by the law unless a registrar is present or the couple then go to a registry office for a civil ceremony.
- A wedding in a registry office with no Church wedding is not officially a Christian marriage as understood by the Catholic Church.

2.2 The Sacrament of Marriage

What is the purpose of Christian marriage?

Marriage and love in the Bible

Genesis (Genesis 2:18 and 2:4), says it is normal for a man and a woman to leave their parents and come together as one in loving companionship and bring new life into the word and raise children in a loving family: 'Be fruitful and increase in number' (Genesis 1:28). Jesus repeats this when he says 'But at the beginning of creation God made them male and female. For this reason a man will leave his father and mother and be united to his wife, and the two will become one flesh. So they are no longer two, but one.' (Mark 10:6–8) Marriage is about the love of the couple, the love of new life and the love of God. It is a calling. God calls people to marriage.

A sacrament

The Catholic Church teaches that marriage is a calling or vocation, and a **sacrament**, a sacred sign showing inward grace, that God is really present in a special way. Marriage is a way of sharing life and love in companionship. The Holy Spirit, which is present in all the sacraments, helps them grow in mutual love. Jesus celebrated at the wedding of Cana with a miracle. (John 2:1–11)

A *Created for companionship*

The nature of Christian marriage

What is the ideal of Christian marriage?

The Roman Catholic Church teaches that the love between men and women should reflect the love of God, a love that supports and comforts. They should love each other 'as Christ loves the Church' (Ephesians 5:24).

Objectives

Know and understand biblical teachings on marriage and love.

Describe what is meant when Christians say marriage is a sacrament.

Suggest and explore what is meant by Christian marriage – its purpose, aims and nature.

Key terms

Sacraments: rites and rituals through which the believer receives a special gift of grace, e.g. baptism or the Eucharist. Roman Catholics believe that sacraments are 'outward signs' of 'inward grace'. Different Christian traditions celebrate different sacraments.

Christian Marriage: when a man and a woman come together and promise to live together in a lifelong, permanent and exclusive relationship.

Permanent: lasting or remaining without essential change.

Exclusive: not divided or shared with others.

Life-giving: having the power to give life.

∞links

Look back at the gifts and fruits of the Holy Spirit on pages 10–11.

Extension activity

Read the miracle of Cana in John 2:11. What does it reveal about Jesus' view of marriage?

Christian marriage is:

1 A lifelong **permanent** love: the commitment is one that lasts until death.

2 An **exclusive** faithful love: the two people are completely faithful to one another. In marriage the couple promise to belong to one another and to continue to work at belonging to one another.

3 **Life-giving**: marriage should be open to new life and the bringing up of a Christian family.

Love in marriage

At the centre of Christian marriage is the command to love of one for another. In Christian marriage:

- they should share the joys and delights of each other and share in one another's happiness, not just their own

- the couple must learn to forgive one another and show reconciliation as they meet with the problems of daily life

- they must bring healing to one another. The difficulties and pain of daily life can be restored and repaired in marriage.

In these ways a married couple reflect the love of a neighbour in an intimate and special way. They are focused on the good of the other. Married life and love should be reciprocal; that is, there should be a mutual sharing between husband and wife of the benefits and difficulties of marriage. It is not enough for one person to do the loving and caring while the other just enjoys the benefits.

Case study

Some reflections on marriage

66 *At the end of a difficult day, when everything has gone wrong at work, just to have someone to be there with me, to listen without judging, to soothe me and to comfort me. Maybe even get things back into perspective and help me remember what really matters in life.* 99

66 *You need to learn to say sorry and learn to mean it, and learn to accept sorry from the other side. You can't spend so much time close to someone who really matters, without messing up sometimes and if you can't deal with forgiveness, how can you move on together?* 99

66 *The pain that we have to suffer in life is that bit easier because someone else is there with us.* 99

66 *After years and years of being together, suddenly you see something new about yourself, and in your partner ... and you realise that the journey is still only just beginning.* 99

Summary

You should now understand that the Christian idea of marriage is based on biblical teaching. The Church teaches that marriage is a sacrament, a sign of God's love, and that it should be a permanent, exclusive and life-giving relationship of love.

Activity

1 What beliefs about Christian marriage can be found in the following teaching?

66 *... each man should have his own wife, and each woman her own husband. The husband should fulfil his marital duty to his wife, and likewise the wife to her husband. The wife's body does not belong to her alone but also to her husband. In the same way, the husband's body does not belong to him alone but also to his wife.* 99

1 Corinthians 7:2–4

AQA Examiner's tip

Makes sure you are clear on the three things that the Church teaches about marriage, that it is loving, committed and lifelong, which is exclusive to one person and open to new life.

Activities

2 In what ways can a couple bring healing to each other?

3 How is sharing in each other's happiness close to Jesus's teaching of love?

4 What do you think the Bible means when it says that a husband's body is no longer his own but his wife's? And why might that be important?

5 In what ways can it be said that marriage is a sacrament?

5 What do the reflections suggest to about the couples who expressed them.

The conditions of marriage

Marriage is so important that there are conditions required by the Catholic Church:

- Marriage must be freely chosen (not just because parents want it, or because the bride is pregnant).
- The bride and groom must be free to marry (not already married). If one of the couple is married to someone else, they are not free.
- The marriage should be open to the possibility of having children.
- The bride and groom should have a responsible attitude to marriage and understand that it is a sacrament, a covenant (an agreement) and an equal loving relationship.

Marriage preparation

In the Roman Catholic Church, couples attend marriage preparation classes with a priest. This is a chance for them to think through why they want to get married and what Christian marriage involves. Are they really prepared to stay together in times of hardship such as illness? Do they have any reservations they need to talk through?

A Marriage preparation is a chance to think things through

Misconceptions about marriage

The bride and bridegroom marry each other. The priest is a witness of the Church and God, and leads the celebration of the sacrament but he does not **do** the marrying. The people who come to celebrate the marriage are witnesses but they are also invited to support the couple for the rest of their lives.

Objectives

Know the different parts of the rite of marriage, explain what they mean and why they are important.

Recall the conditions for a Catholic marriage and explain why Christians believe they are important.

Suggest reasons why marriage needs preparation.

Activities

1   Think of two specific examples of situations where a marriage is not freely entered into.

2   Why does it matter whether the bride and groom fully understand what marriage involves?

Key terms

Rite: a set pattern of words and actions, for example those which are used in the celebration of the sacraments.

Vows: solemn promises that are made, usually with God and people as witnesses.

Activities

3   'Why just prepare for marriage? Why not also spend some time during the marriage getting advice and support from others as well?' Explain why a Christian might argue that this is true?

4   How might a Church community support the marriages within it?

B   *The marriage rite*

Part of the rite	Description	Explanation
Welcome and purpose of marriage	The priest welcomes all those who have come to the Church wedding and reminds everyone what marriage is.	The people who have come: ■ are witnesses to the marriage ■ have a duty to support the couple throughout their life, not just on the day. Marriage is: ■ a sacrament so God is involved ■ lifelong.
The Liturgy of the Word (Readings)	Readings from the Bible and the priest speaks for a short while.	This is to remind people about: ■ the sacrament of Christian marriage ■ the dignity of wedded love ■ the grace of the sacrament ■ the responsibilities of married people.
Questions	The priest asks questions of the couple before they marry.	This is to ensure that the couple: ■ have undertaken marriage freely and without reservation ■ will honour and love each other for ever ■ will leave their marriage open to children (unless the couple are advanced in years).
Consent/ Exchange of vows	The priest asks 'N, do you take N to be your wife/husband? Do you promise to be true to him/her in good times and in bad, in sickness and in health, to love him/her and honour him/her all the days of your life?' to which the reply is 'I do.' Then the husband and wife say to each other 'I, N, take you, N, for my lawful wife/husband, to have and to hold, from this day forward, for better, for worse, for richer, for poorer, in sickness and in health, until death do us part.'	The vows express the Christian beliefs about marriage, that it should be: ■ loving ■ lifelong ■ supporting in all times ■ faithful (exclusive). Although the priest asks questions and acts as a witness it is the couple who marry each other, and confer the sacrament on each other not the priest.
Exchange of rings	'Take this ring as a sign of my love and fidelity.'	The rings symbolise the unending nature of marriage. Fidelity (faithfulness) refers to marriage being exclusive.
Prayers and nuptial blessing	Prayers are said and a blessing is given.	To: ■ ask God's blessing on the marriage ■ ask that God will unite the couple in love forever ■ ask that they may be companions to one another ■ ask that they may have children and a happy old age.
Communion	The sacrament of the Eucharist is received.	The sacrament will strengthen the marriage by bringing Christ into the couple's lives.
Signing of the register	The newlyweds and two witnesses sign the marriage registry.	To make the marriage recognised as a civil marriage, as well as a sacramental one.

Extension activity

Look at Table B and then, using pages 26–28, find teachings which relate to the different aspects of the service, and readings that might be appropriate for the Liturgy of the Word section. (You could make your own version of this table and add your new information into an extra column.)

Summary

You should now know that Christian marriage needs preparation to make sure the couple understand what it means and consider the future, and that it must be entered into freely. The marriage rite reflects Christian beliefs about marriage.

AQA   *Examiner's tip*

Remember that it is not enough just to know what happens in the service, you need to understand the symbols of marriage as well.

2.4 Parenthood

The importance of family life

The Church teaches that the family is where society begins. Healthy and happy families help build a healthy and happy society. The family is the church at home, a community of faith, hope and love which supports the Church as a whole. The family is a place where members learn to share feelings, loves and interests and a place where the young, sick and elderly can be cared for. It is also where children first learn about Christian life.

The duties in family life

The Church teaches that both children and parents have responsibilities to one another which must be balanced. Parents have a particular responsibility in making sure they show love, care and understanding to their children, as well as proper attention to the upbringing of children.

A   Family duties

Children	Parents
Should respect parents out of thanks for the life, love and work of parents which has brought children into the world to help them grow and fully develop in stature, wisdom and love	Should respect children as persons of human dignity, and as a gift and not a piece of property. Must also respect God's call for their children and not hold them back
Should be obedient to parents	Are responsible for spiritual and moral education of their children, so they may act responsibly and grow in their faith
Should show love towards and respect for brothers and sisters	Must provide children with a suitable home and be good examples

Objectives

Describe and explain Catholic teachings on the importance of family life.

Know and understand Christian teachings on the duties of children and parents to each other.

Beliefs and teachings

Children

Children, obey your parents – for this is right. Honour your father and your mother – which is the first commandment with a promise – that it may go well with you and that you may enjoy long life on earth. Fathers, do not exasperate your children, instead bring them up in the training and correction of the Lord.

Ephesians 6:1–4

Beliefs and teachings

Thus the home is the first school of Christian life.

Catechism 1657

B *Family life*

Activities

1 What do these two quotations suggest about the way these parents are trying to fulfil their Christian duties? Suggest why these phrases are not good statements about parental duties to children. Try to improve both sentences.

   a Why might children find it difficult to listen to their parents' advice sometimes?

   b 'I just make sure I drag them to church each Sunday!' (Parent A)
   'It's not for me to tell them what to do with their lives; I leave it up to them.' (Parent B)

Beliefs and teachings

Parents

Parents must regard their children as children of God and respect them as human persons … A child is not something owed to one, but is a gift. The 'supreme gift of marriage' is a human person. A child may not be considered a piece of property …

Catechism 2222, 2378

Case study

The challenges of parenthood

'It's hard to explain what life is like after children. Before, your time is yours. You can pop out whenever you like, you just think about yourself and your wife. After your child is born, everything centres around them – their needs, their illnesses, their hopes and joys. When you hold your baby for the first time in your hands it's like something more precious than all the money in the world. You watch them grow and everything they learn to do is amazing to watch. Whenever you make a decision about anything, they are the first thing to be thought about. Will it be ok for them or not? Your time goes to them – if you are very, very lucky you occasionally get a bit of time for yourself … and I mean a bit.

And you worry – all the time. I remember when my baby was seriously ill and on a life support machine. It was like my heart was there … attached to the machine – I wanted to swap places for her but couldn't. When they enjoy life and shout for joy you feel their happiness and you take pleasure in their happiness. It is the most powerful thing you can imagine. The love you show them is multiplied back in you. Of course I worry about what happens when they grow up, and sometimes they drive me absolutely crazy. But you just have to swallow that up. That's just children.'

A father reflecting on parenthood

C *What do you think this photo says about the family relationships? What could help in this situation?*

Extension activity

Discuss with a partner your own views on having children. Do you want to? Give reasons for your answer.

Activities

2   In your own words, what are the duties of parents and children according to Christian teaching?

3   Why, according to the Bible, should children honour their parents?

4   In what ways might parents fail to provide a good example to their children?

Summary

You should now know that the Church teaches that the family is the first place for learning about God's love and that children and parents have important duties to each other.

AQA   *Examiner's tip*

Remember that there are duties on both sides between parents and children.

2.5 Adoption and fostering

How the Church supports family life

Here are some ways in which the family of the Church can support the family:

- schools to support education of children of a Roman Catholic community
- welcoming families to Mass with special facilities for children and a warm and positive approach to having children in the church
- special services for children and church groups for children
- national charities dedicated to supporting family life such as Catholic Marriage Care
- resources to help support marriages including days of reflection focused on couples and Catholic Marriage Counselling services
- social events organised for families to do things together.

Children in need

Difficulties at home such as illness, relationship problems, family breakdown or circumstances in which a child is threatened can all lead to a child being removed from their home and looked after by social services.

A

Fostering	Looking after someone else's child in your own home for a period of time. Foster parents work with social services to give a child a chance to have an ordinary family life. They sometimes work to try to re-unite a child and birth family or, if this is not possible, help them to live in a more stable alternative family.
Adoption	Taking on all the legal parental rights and responsibilities for the child in a lifelong commitment through good times and bad. Children may be adopted when their own parents cannot care for them any more.

Many children who need to be looked after have suffered emotional harm. They may feel a sense of loss of their family. They may have had to move homes many times in their lives.

Objectives

Examine how the Church can support family life.

Explore adoption and fostering and explain the differences between them.

Consider the qualities needed for adoptive or foster parents and the different reasons why Christians may wish to adopt or foster a child.

Key terms

Fostering: the taking of a child from a different family into a family home and bringing them up with the rest of the new family.

Adoption: the legal process where a person (child) is taken (adopted) into the family as a son or daughter.

Extension activity

Carry out an audit of a local Roman Catholic Church to see what sorts of provision it makes for families (this could be done by looking at the Church notice board, looking at some parish newsletters or the church website). Suggest areas for improvement.

What qualities are needed to look after children?

- a commitment to a child
- the ability to accept a child's past and to help the child to do so
- the ability to make relationships with children
- a sense of humour
- some support from family, friends and other networks
- a flexible, patient, open-minded approach
- a willingness to encourage and support children to keep in contact with members of their birth family where appropriate
- a willingness to work with the child's social worker and other agencies that may be involved such as teachers, psychologists and other specialists.

Before you can foster or adopt a child, you have to pass through an important process that checks your suitability for caring for these very special children. This includes being appraised by a social worker, who will also speak to your doctor and other people who know you.

Reasons why Christians may put themselves forward for fostering and adoption

A Christian couple may choose to look after children by fostering or adoption because:

- They may feel moved by the presence of so many children who do not have parents to care for them and decide that fostering or adoption is one way they can live a life of love for others, and make a difference to them.
- They may be unable to have children of their own for medical reasons and choose to express their generosity by caring for children who are in need.
- They may feel that they have had a fortunate life with good family support and want to share this with others.

B *How is adoption a commitment?*

Summary

You should now know that the family of the Church can offer support to families in many ways. Christians may feel that fostering and adoption are good ways of showing love for those in need, and sharing what they have with others.

Activities

1   Role play an interview at an adoption agency.

   Decide what sorts of questions a couple should be asked and think about what answers the agency might hope for.

2   a   Explain in your own words why a Christian couple might wish to foster or adopt a child.

   b   What beliefs might influence them?

AQA   *Examiner's tip*

Remember that there are specific reasons why Christians may wish to foster or adopt children, but some reasons would be shared by many couples.

2.6   Sex outside marriage

Change in society

Sex outside marriage includes sex between people who are in a casual relationship as well as those who are unfaithful. There has been a considerable change in attitudes towards sexual relationships in the last 60 years. The availability of artificial contraception and the legal access to abortion, along with greater freedom, has meant that people feel safer about having sex outside marriage.

Research on sexual behaviour in Britain today suggests it is common for people to have sexual relationships outside marriage and most people have sex before they get married although generally people have very strong views that sexual unfaithfulness to a partner is wrong.

Sex outside marriage

The Church's teaching on sex is based on the biblical teaching on love. Sex outside a Christian marriage is described in the Bible as 'fornication'. The Bible teaches that it is wrong and a sign of sin (see Matthew 15:19).

Anyone outside Christian marriage should live by chastity (sexual restraint). This includes single people who have never been married, widows, and homosexual couples.

Christian arguments against sex outside marriage

The Bible, which many Christians believe should be obeyed as it is the word of God, teaches against sex outside marriage. The Church teaches that the human body is precious and important (a 'temple of the Holy Spirit' says St Paul). Sex outside marriage is wrong and Roman Catholics are asked to follow this teaching as part of their faith.

People who believe and follow these teachings from the Bible and the Church might use the following arguments.

A *Christian arguments against sex outside marriage*

In search of the greatest love	The best possible love is one that will always be there (permanent), will always be committed to you (faithful) and one which is open to God (the possibility of new life).
	A love which is closed off from God, only temporary or not offered to you alone, is not as great a love and does not support family life.
The failings of sex outside marriage	Casual sex expresses little love. It is a momentary encounter with little concern for the future or the other person. It does not respect the sexual act as a special expression of lifelong love and commitment to someone.
	Serial monogamy shows only a temporary commitment to the other person. It will not support a couple through the ups and downs of life. It only lasts until the next person comes along.
	Living together is not as much of a commitment as marriage.
	If a child is born it may not receive the stability of family life as it is growing up.

Alternative views

Many people have a different view on sex outside marriage. Here are some arguments they might use:

- Sex is simply a casual expression of love which people should be able to freely offer to anyone who wants it. We should be free to enjoy bodily pleasures.
- You should stay faithful to the person you are currently with but you don't need marriage. You may have several partners in turn. This is known as serial monogamy.
- As divorce is common, you should be able to have a trial period of living as a couple to see if you get on with each other before deciding to get married. This is known as 'living together'.
- Weddings are too expensive and draw attention away from the loving relationship. Marriage seems to be more about the law, a party and a piece of paper than the relationship. You don't need these things to have a good relationship.

Misconceptions

People sometimes think that religion is against sex. This is wrong. God has given sex as a wonderful gift for a couple in a loving, permanent and exclusive relationship. It is a way new life can come into the world.

Living together: some practical problems

Research suggests that many people believe that living together gives you the same rights as marriage. They believe in something called 'common-law marriage'. However this is not true in the UK.

Unmarried couples, even if they have children, have far fewer legal protections. So if one leaves or dies, the surviving partner will not automatically be treated in the same way as if they had been married. This can affect inheritance, home ownership, and guardianship of any children from a previous relationship. They may not benefit from their partner's pension.

∞links

Look back at Chapter 1, Christian values, to remind yourself of Christian beliefs about love.

B   *Unmarried couples have less legal protection*

Activities

Working alone or in groups:

1. Draw up a table showing arguments for and against sex outside marriage. Use the information from these pages to identity as many arguments as possible with reasons to support each argument.
2. Using the information in your table make the strongest possible argument against sex outside marriage and for sex outside marriage **from a Christian point of view**. Decide whether each argument is fully convincing or only partly convincing.

Beliefs and teachings

Keep away from sexual immorality. All other sins that someone commit are done outside the body; the sexually immoral person sins against his own body. Do you not realise that your body is the temple of the Holy Spirit, who is in you and whom you received from God? You are not your own property, then; you have been bought at a price. So use your body for the glory of God.

1 Corinthians 6:18–20

AQA   *Examiner's tip*

The reasons for the Church's teaching that sex outside marriage is wrong are directly linked to the three beliefs about the nature of Christian marriage (see page 27).

Summary

You should be able to explain that Christian teachings hold that sex outside marriage is wrong and the belief that love should be permanent, committed and open to new life, not temporary, casual or selfish.

Marital breakdown

Marital breakdown

Marital breakdown can cause a great deal of distress for the couple and any children. When a marriage fails, it is the failure of something that everyone involved placed their hope in. It can lead to argument, upset and a profound sense of loss. It causes instability which can be very difficult for children. It can also bring the parents much unhappiness, anxiety and loss of confidence.

What causes difficulties in marriage?

There are many different causes of tension in marriage. These include:

- the loss of the early romance (being in love)
- immaturity, excessive drinking and domestic violence
- an inability to have children
- the loss of a child
- work and money difficulties
- disappointment about lovemaking, especially if the couple give little attention to each other's feelings
- ill health, for example if a child or spouse becomes seriously ill or disabled
- unfaithfulness
- the lack of awareness of each other's problems because of the distractions of work or family.

A Tensions

What can be done to prevent marital breakdown?

All marriages go through difficult times but many couples do not seek out help when they are having difficulty. They may feel embarrassed about discussing their marriage. They may feel that it is their private life and has nothing to do with other people. Left unaddressed, the problems can get worse.

Good marriage preparation

It is important for couples to be well prepared for the changes that will come about in marriage. All couples who wish to marry in Catholic Churches must attend marriage preparation classes, which are usually run by the Parish. Good preparation can help prevent misunderstandings at the start of the marriage which could cause difficulties later. The priest can provide support and advice to couples.

Good communication

One of the most important aspects of marriage is communication. This means talking honestly about problems, desires, goals and feelings. When they are not discussed openly, small worries or disagreements that could be resolved through a conversation can seem to become extremely important and frustrating, which can damage a couple's relationship. Couples who divorce later in life often comment that they just 'drifted apart'; this loss of love could be avoided in many cases if the couple spent time on their friendship by talking to each other.

External help

There are many ways in which the Church supports couples and family life:

- Priests give advice to couples experiencing difficulties in their marriage as well as providing the Sacrament of Reconciliation to encourage forgiveness where harm has been done.
- Marriage Care, a Christian charity, works to support lifelong Christian marriage. The organisation provides relationship counselling, help and advice.
- Local parish churches often run special family days to support family life.
- The Catenian Association is a fellowship of men dedicated to supporting family life through faith.
- As with all difficulties in life, Christians are encouraged to pray for help to overcome them, and to receive the sacraments to gain spiritual strength.

links

For more about preparation before marriage, see page 28.

Activities

2   Why could it be argued that good marriage preparation is essential?

3   Create an action plan for a Parish Church to provide support for marriages. Look back at the list of difficulties that couples face on page 36. What sort of social and spiritual support could a parish offer?

4   What advice do you think should be given to young people thinking about marriage? What advice can you give about what couples can do to help (a) prevent difficulties in the first place and (b) overcome difficulties?

Extension activity

Find out more about Marriage Care at www.marriagecare.org.uk and The Catenian Association at www.thecatenianassociation.org.

AQA   Examiner's tip

Remember that there are ways of preventing marriage breakdown as well as help being available for when marriages are experiencing difficulties.

Summary

You should now be able to show an understanding that most marriages face difficulties at some time, but that there are things couples can do to help prevent marriage break-up.

Divorce in England and Wales

In 1969 The Divorce Reform Act made divorce much easier than before in the UK. Today, many marriages in Britain break down. In the UK there were 144,220 divorces in 2007. **Divorce** is a civil procedure which legally recognises that there is no longer a marriage between a couple. Divorce in England and Wales is possible for marriages of more than one year, when they have irretrievably broken down. Law Courts include adultery, unreasonable behaviour, two years' separation or desertion as justifications for divorce.

Roman Catholic teaching on divorce, remarriage and annulment

Divorce and remarriage

The Roman Catholic Church teaches that divorce cannot dissolve a valid marriage between two baptised people. Marriage is a solemn agreement and a sacrament. It is permanent, exclusive and lifelong and in the wedding ceremony Christians are asked to freely agree to this (or to give their 'consent'). In the New Testament Jesus said that to divorce and get married again is to commit adultery against the first person you married. St Paul says that a husband and wife should not get divorced. The Roman Catholic Church teaches that divorce is damaging to family life and society.

> ### Beliefs and teachings
>
> Therefore what God has joined together, let man not separate.
>
> *Mark* 10:9
>
> Anyone who divorces his wife and marries another woman commits adultery against her.
>
> *Mark* 10:11
>
> A wife must not separate from her husband. But if she does she must remain unmarried or else be reconciled to her husband. And a husband must not divorce his wife.
>
> *1 Corinthians* 7:10–11
>
> Divorce is immoral also because it introduces disorder into the family and into society.
>
> *Catechism* 2385

Remarriage cannot take place in a Catholic church because of vows promising to stay together 'until death do us part'. Marriage is a sacrament and sacraments have a permanent effect. Second marriages after a divorce are not recognised by the Catholic Church. The couple's first marriage is still recognised and the second is considered to be adultery. This is a grave sin and so the couple cannot receive communion.

Objectives

Explore Roman Catholic teaching on divorce, giving reasons for that teaching.

Explain the difference between divorce and annulment and suggest why some Christians disagree with the Church's teaching.

A

Key terms

Divorce: legal ending of a marriage.

Re-marriage: when people who have been married before marry again.

Annulment: when the Roman Catholic Church declares a marriage invalid. Various conditions must be met to prove this. For example, if one of the couple was unable to understand the demands of being married.

B *Separation*

Separation

The separation of a couple is permitted in the event of emotional or physical danger (e.g. from domestic violence). The marriage is still valid so **re-marriage** is not permissible. A Roman Catholic in this situation may get a civil divorce and choose to live a single life.

Annulment

Annulment is not a Roman Catholic version of divorce. Annulment is the decision of the Church that the sacrament of marriage was not present when the vows were made. A Church Marriage Tribunal considers the request and investigates the circumstances. Situations which may lead to an annulment being granted include:

- where one or both were forced into the marriage
- where one or both never intended to have children
- where one refuses to show any love or care for the other. An example of this would be if, once married, one partner changes completely, suggesting the vows were not made in good faith.

Annulment recognises that consent was not fully or properly given at the time the vows were made. Those who have had their marriage annulled can marry again as the first marriage was declared invalid.

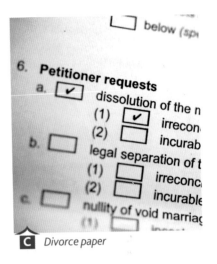

C *Divorce paper*

Debates about divorce and remarriage in Christianity

Some Christians argue that divorce should be accepted in certain circumstances, such as in the case of domestic violence or abuse against the children or adultery. Other Christians argue that there is a need to accept that human beings make mistakes and that God is a forgiving God and would want people to be forgiven and have another opportunity for happiness.

One reason for this difference is a disagreement over the interpretation Jesus's teaching in Matthew 5:27–32.

Beliefs and teachings

Anyone who divorces his wife, except for marital unfaithfulness, causes her to become an adulteress, and anyone who marries the divorced woman commits adultery.

Matthew 5:27–32

Some argue that this means Jesus was allowing divorce in the case of adultery. The Roman Catholic Church suggests that the word 'adultery' here means 'illicit marriage' – a marriage which never should have happened because, for instance, one or both of the couple were not free to marry, did not freely enter into marriage, were not old enough to give consent, or were too closely related.

Summary

You should now know the Roman Catholic Church opposes divorce, and re-marriage after divorce.

Activities

1 Explain the differences between divorce and annulment.

2 Why does the Church teach that divorce is wrong?

3 Explain why 'consent' is important in Roman Catholic teaching on divorce and annulment?

4 Why might some of the teachings on divorce be difficult for people to accept?

5 How can the Church provide support, love and healing for those whose marriages have broken down?

6 Devise a flow diagram to show the Church's teaching on divorce, separation and annulment.

AQA Examiner's tip

Make sure you can explain why annulment is not a Catholic version of divorce.

2

Christian marriage – summary

For the examination you should now be able to:

✔ explain the terms Christian marriage, annulment, divorce, remarriage

✔ explain what is meant by saying that marriage is a sacrament

✔ explain the purposes and nature of Christian marriage

✔ outline the rite of marriage, including the symbolism, explaining how it relates to Christian beliefs about marriage

✔ explain how important Christians believe family life to be and what is meant by responsible parenthood

✔ explain why Christians believe that the fostering and adoption of children is important

✔ understand Roman Catholic Teaching with reference to sexual relationships outside marriage

✔ outline the causes of marital breakdown and what can be done to prevent it

✔ understand the impact of Roman Catholic teachings on the lifestyle and attitudes of the believer.

Sample answer

1 Write an answer to the following exam question.

Explain the meaning and importance of marriage in the Roman Catholic Church. *(6 marks)*

2 Read the following sample answer:

> For Catholics, marriage is forever. You are not allowed to get divorced. Jesus taught that no one should split up a marriage. You should not be unfaithful by having affairs with anyone. You should also try to have children because new life is really important. Marriage should be loving, like Jesus loved the Church.

3 With a partner, discuss the sample answer. Do you think that there are other things that the student could have included in the answer?

4 What mark would you give this answer out of 6? Look to the mark scheme in the Introduction on page 7 (AO1). What are the reasons for the mark you have given?

AQA Examination-style questions

1   Look at the photograph and answer the following questions.

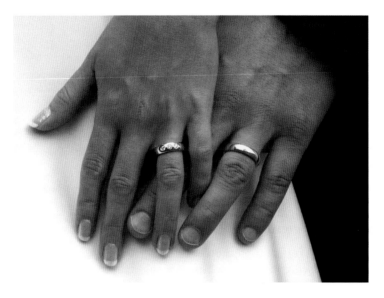

(a)   What do the wedding rings symbolise for Christians?   *(2 marks)*

(b)   Explain the meaning and importance of marriage in the Roman Catholic Church.   *(6 marks)*

(c)   Explain why Roman Catholics support adoption and fostering.   *(4 marks)*

(d)   'There is no difference between divorce and annulment.'
Do you agree? Give reasons for your answer, showing that you have thought about
more than one point of view. Refer to Roman Catholic teaching in your answer.   *(6 marks)*

   Remember that you need to give specific reasons for each point of view. Try to link those
reasons to teachings or beliefs.

3 Christian vocation

3.1 An introduction to Christian vocation and the Parable of the Talents

▉ What is vocation?

Vocation is the calling of God to every human being (vocation means calling). In the Old Testament God repeatedly called people to do his will, for instance Abraham and Moses, and repeatedly calls Israel, his people, to come back to him. Mark's Gospel begins with a calling 'A voice cries in the wilderness, prepare the way for the Lord' which John the Baptist responds to. Jesus called the disciples to follow him, leaving their work and family and living as he lived, so Christians believe that Jesus calls them to follow him.

How is Christian vocation different from other vocations

Anyone may feel called to take up a certain profession or role in life. Someone may feel called to be a doctor or a teacher. These callings may in some way be connected to a Christian calling to serve others, but Christian vocation is not about being successful or achieving great things in work and life. Christian vocation is fundamentally a call from God, which asks for a person to serve God and serve others, to love God and love others.

▉ The Parable of the Talents (Matthew 25:14–30)

Objectives

Express in different ways, the meaning of the phrase Christian vocation.

Recall and analyse of the Parable of the Talents.

Key terms

Vocation: doing something for the love of it; a feeling that God is calling someone to a special ministry or way of serving others.

Talents: qualities, attributes or abilities which in Christian belief are gifts from God and should be used in his service.

Beliefs and teachings

Again, it will be like a man going on a journey, who called his servants and entrusted his property to them. To one he gave five talents of money, to another two talents, and to another one talent, each according to his ability. Then he went on his journey. The man who had received the five talents went at once and put his money to work and gained five more. So also, the one with the two talents gained two more. But the man who had received the one talent went off, dug a hole in the ground and hid his master's money.

After a long time the master of those servants returned and settled accounts with them. The man who had received the five talents brought the other five. 'Master,' he said, 'you entrusted me with five talents. See, I have gained five more.' His master replied, 'Well done, good and faithful servant! You have been faithful with a few things; I will put you in charge of many things. Come and share your master's happiness!'

The man with the two talents also came. 'Master,' he said, 'you entrusted me with two talents; see, I have gained two more.' His master replied, 'Well done, good and faithful servant! You have been faithful with a few things; I will put you in charge of many things. Come and share your master's happiness!'

Then the man who had received the one talent came. 'Master,' he said, 'I knew that you are a hard man, harvesting where you have not sown and gathering where you have not scattered seed. So I was afraid and went out and hid your talent in the ground. See, here is what belongs to you.'

His master replied, 'You wicked, lazy servant! So you knew that I harvest where I have not sown and gather where I have not scattered seed? Well then, you should have put my money on deposit with the bankers, so that when I returned, I would have received it back with interest.

Take the talent from him and give it to the one who has the ten talents. For everyone who has will be given more, and he will have an abundance. Whoever does not have, even what he has will be taken from him. And throw that worthless servant outside, into the darkness, where there will be weeping and gnashing of teeth.

Matthew 25:14–30

Interpreting the Parable of the Talents

There are different ways of interpreting this parable:

- Although **talents** meant currency in New Testament times, modern interpretations understand the word talent to mean abilities, gifts or aptitude.
- It could be suggesting that people should use the gifts they have been given to live responsibly, in view of the Last Judgement which will come.
- It may also be suggesting that it is really important to live an active and productive life, rather than being lazy.

■ Alternatives for Christian calling

There are three ways for Christians to respond to God's call in the Catholic Church. These are shown in Diagram **A**.

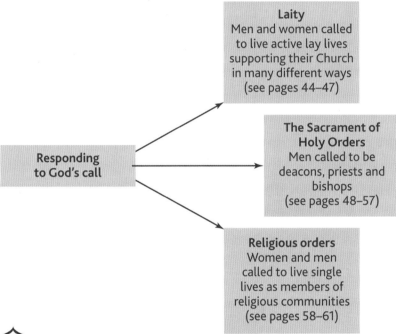

A   *Three ways for Christians to respond to God's call in the Catholic Church*

Activities

1. Look at all of the information on these pages and give three different examples of what is meant by 'vocation'.
2. What do you think is the main message of the Parable of the Talents and why?

AQA   *Examiner's tip*

Remember that there are different ways in which people can use their talents and gifts, and this chapter includes different examples of them.

Summary

You should now understand that the Church teaches that all are called to follow in Christ's footsteps and that this is a challenging undertaking but is part of the responsibility a Christian has of using their gifts in a productive and holy life.

3.2 The role and vocation of lay people (laity) in the Roman Catholic Church

What is the vocation of lay people?

The laity (or **lay people**) are people who have been baptised into the Church but do not take holy orders (such as being a priest or a nun). Obviously, the laity make up most of the members of the Catholic Church. The laity have important responsibilities, these are:

- to live their lives according to Christian teachings, including social, political and economic aspects of their lives
- to be animators of human society (bringing their faith into ordinary human life)
- to form a community that is recognised as the people of God.

Beliefs and teachings

Lay Christians ... they have the right and duty, individually or grouped in associations, to work so that the divine message of salvation may be known and accepted by all men throughout the earth.

Catechism 900

Objectives

Explain what is meant by the vocation of lay people.

Give different examples of parish groups which demonstrate Christian vocation in action.

Key terms

Lay people (laity): members of the Church who are not in holy orders.

Research activity

Catholic gap years

Young Catholics thinking about taking a gap year between school and further study or work, or after university, may take a Catholic Gap Year (www.catholicgapyear.com/). These offer them opportunities to work and use their talents in a Church-based environment. They offer a way for young people to explore their vocation. Explore the website and read testimonials from those who have done so.

Activity

1 What sort of things bring animation of human life and what sorts of things take it away?

People bring many different gifts, services and ways of working to the Church and to human life. Christian vocation is a calling to be involved in both Church life and broader human life. Look at the parish notices on page 45 taken from a Catholic parish website, for an illustration of the kinds of work that lay people in the Catholic Church might be involved in.

A

B

C

Parish notices

Youth Group

We have a small but vibrant youth group which meets monthly. Each meeting revolves around 'Faith, Fun and Food'. We have planned Youth Masses, welcomed CAFOD speakers to tell us about Fairtrade as well as visits to Walsingham. Some of the group are planning to go to Cologne for the World Youth Event with the Pope. It is possible to go as a young helper to Lourdes in August each year and some of the group are on the Bishop's Diocesan Youth Council.

Parent & Toddler Group

The group meets in the Club Friday mornings 09.15–10.45 (term time only). This is an ideal opportunity for toddlers to meet and play together under the watchful eye of their parents, whilst the parents themselves have a chance to make friends over a cup of tea. There is also an opportunity for parents with toddlers to attend Mass together to help the children share in Mass which is planned especially for them. Details will be published in the weekly Parish newsletter.

Association for the Propagation of the Faith (APF)

The APF is a world wide missionary organisation that provides Bishops in missionary areas with additional funds where these are not available from other sources. In our parish we have over 100 members, and nine promoters who deliver the magazines to members four times a year, collect the donations and empty the collecting boxes one or more times a year as requested. Members also pray for the missions. There are no meetings for this group, the commitment is financial and through prayer.

Society of St Vincent de Paul (SVP)

The SVP is a world wide lay organisation of Christian men and women. The members meet regularly in order to help those in need in a personal way. They visit at home, in care homes and in hospitals. They convey people to the Over 60s Club, Mass, Gatehouse groups, hospitals, shopping and generally meet the needs of people referred to them. The group meets regularly in the Presbytery, the dates and times are published in the weekly newsletter.

CAFOD group

It is this group's aim to tackle issues of injustice, ranging from Third World Debt to easing the burden of individual communities across the world. The work of the group is closely linked with CAFOD's aims and those of JUSTRAID.

Guild of St Martha

Our members serve our parish by helping to keep the church clean and maintained so that when we pray we are in a welcoming and prayerful environment. We have members of all ages, both male and female. We each have an area of the church to look after and always finish with coffee and biscuits. New members are always welcome.

Discussion Group for Questioning Catholics

Are you a Lapsed Catholic? A Questioning Catholic? A Doubting Catholic? Then we have a discussion group for you! We meet in the Club, under the church, on the last Wednesday of each month at 19.30. Come and express your views. Open to young and old alike, male and female. Your views make the agenda!

Third World Group

The group aims, through fundraising events, to support projects set up by missionaries in Third World Countries such as Ghana, Brazil, Peru, Ecuador and Zimbabwe. The projects are mainly in healthcare and education. The Group meet each month in the Presbytery. Various fundraising events are held throughout the year including Dances, Lenten lunches, cake stalls, coffee mornings and Christmas market stalls.

From the notice board of the parish of St Edmund in Bury St Edmund

---

Activity

2 Look at the notices in the Case study. How do you think they show Christians living out their vocation?

Extension activity

Research what is going on in your own local parish church.

Summary

You should now understand that lay people play an important part in many aspects of Church life and their vocation must also inform how they live their lives at home and in public.

AQA Examiner's tip

Make sure you can give different examples of how lay people live a life of vocation.

Lay ministry and the Priesthood of the believer

The Catholic Church teaches that all Christians are called to evangelise, sanctify and transform the world. This means to spread the word of God, to make the world a more holy place and a more moral place. They are part of Christ's priestly, prophetic and royal office or mission. In short it is: 'to spread the Kingdom of Christ over all the earth' (Catechism 863). This is part of what is called **Lay Ministry**. Lay people are called to collaborate with deacons, priests and bishops in the ministry of the Church.

A *The calling of lay people*

The calling of lay people

To witness – share in Christ's priestly office

At baptism and confirmation, Catholics are dedicated to Christ and anointed by the Holy Spirit to ask God that they will be blessed with more fruits of the Spirit. Being a Christian should show in all aspects of life.

As well as these duties, people may have other specific responsibilities, for example:

- parents are called to work for a happy and loving Christian family life at home
- supporting worship: Servers at Church, Eucharistic ministers (distributing Holy Communion), Ministers of the Word (readers)
- lay people may stand in for the priest 'to preside over liturgical prayers, to confer baptism, and to distribute Holy Communion' (Catechism 903).

To teach – share in Christ's prophetic office

Sharing in the prophetic office of Christ means being involved in developing people's faith:

- They have a duty to evangelise (preach the gospel), both to believers and those who do not believe.
- Some lay people support children and adults in their faith journey into the Church through preparation for First Holy Communion, Confirmation and the Rite of Christian Initiation for adults.
- Christians should raise any issues of concern which relate to the good of the Church with priests and bishops. They should also make their opinion known to other Christians.

To lead – share in Christ's kingly office

Lay people are called to participate in the kingly function of Christ. Lay people are called to participate in various ministries at the service of the community including:

- participating in parish councils, diocesan synods, pastoral councils
- the exercise of the pastoral care of a parish, such as taking communion to the sick
- involvement in the good management of the parish finances.

There are also broader responsibilities:

- to work for justice in all aspects of life and to seek to bring moral value into all aspects of human culture and human works
- to keep a balance between their rights and duties as members of human society and rights and duties of members of the Church
- to ensure they are guided by a Christian conscience, in every activity they undertake.

Activity

2 Imagine that a parish bank account is at a bank that invests in countries ruled by dictators and tobacco firms. A member of the parish notices this. What aspect of lay ministry might lead them to action?

Beliefs and teachings

The laity can also feel called, or be in fact called, to cooperate with their pastors in the service of the [church], for the sake of its growth and life.

Catechism 910

Activities

3 A supermarket shelf stacker is asked to work on Sunday. What aspects of Christ's priestly, prophetic and kingly office may come into conflict here?

4 'I do my bit, I go to Mass and put some money in the collection, what more do they want?' In what ways does it sound as though this person has not understood his or her lay ministry?

5 'Religion and politics do not mix'. Why might a Christian disagree with this based on their understanding of their lay ministry?

6 Look back at Photos A, B and C on page 44. Relate the Christian beliefs expressed on this page with the images you can see in the montage.

Summary

You should now understand that the Catholic Church teaches that lay people share in Christ's priestly, prophetic and kingly office with duties and responsibilities affecting all aspects of daily public, private and Church life.

AQA   Examiner's tip

Make sure you are aware of the different kinds of work that lay people are involved with.

3.4 Holy Orders (ordination) and the role of a deacon

Background of Holy Orders

Many ancient civilisations had a man or women responsible for worshipping. Frequently this included making sacrifices to God as well as teaching and handing on traditions. Sometimes this person lived apart from the rest of the community, or had a special position of authority among the people.

Jesus called disciples to follow him and chose twelve to be his **apostles**. The apostles had special authority to cast out unclean spirits and the duties of healing, teaching, preaching and baptising.

Gradually from these early beginnings, the **priesthood** developed. It was given the task of serving the Christian community through teaching and understanding the word of God in the Bible, and the celebration of sacraments.

> **Beliefs and teachings**
>
> Whoever wants to become great among you must be your servant, and whoever wants to be first must be slave of all. For even the Son of Man did not come to be served, but to serve, and to give his life as a ransom for many.
>
> *Mark* 10:42–45

The nature of Holy Orders

The Sacrament of Holy Orders is made up of three different roles:

A

Bishops	Ordination as a bishop confers the fullness of sacrament. This means the bishop is a successor of the apostles, and shares the ruling office with other bishops and the Pope.	A bishop is also a visible head in the Church, and has responsibility for the priests and deacons in his Diocese.
Priests	Ordination as a priest seals the priests with a spiritual character that means he can act in the name of Christ the Head; this confers on him the role of the bishop's assistant, so he can celebrate the sacraments.	He works with the bishop to preach the Gospel, celebrate Mass and to care for the faithful in his parish, as a shepherd cares for his sheep.
Deacons	The deacon is the servant of all, ordained for service to the Church.	He supports a priest in the caring role of the parish with some of the same duties.

Objectives

Give examples of what is meant by the priesthood and how it developed.

Explain what is meant by Holy Orders and the role of the Deacon, and suggest different ways the Deacon serves God and the Church.

Key terms

Apostles: the leaders of the early Church. The word literally means 'sent out'.

Priesthood: the roles and duties of a priest. Central to this is saying Mass.

Deacon/Diaconate: a minister who may lead some services such as baptism and marriage, reads the Gospel at Mass and participate in charity such as visiting the sick.

Extension activity

Read Acts 7, 2:42–47 and 6:1–7. These give us snapshots from the beginnings of the Christian Community. What links can you find between the activity of the Apostles and the role of the deacon and priest today?

In each case the people feel called to serve God and Church in the special ways that each ministry practises. Deacons, priests and bishops feel personally called to serve and this calling is a great source of strength and reassurance for them in meeting the demands of their ministry.

The role of a deacon

A **deacon** may be in full-time employment outside of the Church. He may be single or married. He may be a permanent deacon or he may be in training to be a priest.

There are three main parts to the work of a deacon: liturgy, the word, and charity.

1 **Liturgy**: he may preside at baptisms, weddings, funerals and lead people in prayer.
2 **The word**: he may read the Gospel and preach to others.
3 **Charity**: he serves the need of the people, especially the poor.

The deacon serves the Bishop, who may ask him to carry out additional parish duties, university and prison chaplaincy work, or other social or spiritual work linked to the parish.

Activities

1 Why do you think Christians feel it is important to have people who lead the religious community?

2 a In what ways do deacons serve the Christian community?

   b How do these activities reflect the life of Jesus?

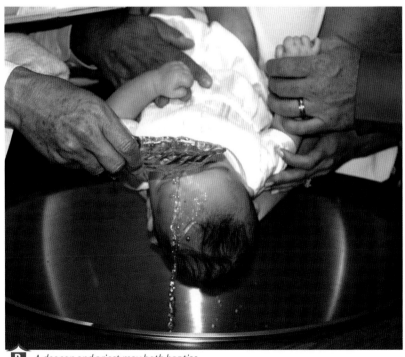

B A deacon and priest may both baptise

∞ links

To find out about the duties of a priest, turn over to pages 50 to 51.

Summary

You should now understand that the priesthood is given the task of serving the Christian community through teaching and understanding the word of God in the Bible, and the celebration of sacraments. Deacons serve God and the Church.

AQA **Examiner's tip**

Make sure you know the differences between the duties of the deacon with those of the priest.

3.5 The role of a priest

The role of a priest

A priest is either under the authority of a bishop or, if he is in religious orders, a superior. In the Western Catholic Church priests are celibate (they do not marry or have sexual relationships with a partner) with only a few exceptions. The role of a priest is to 'preach the Gospel, to shepherd the faithful and to celebrate the divine worship'. (Lumen Gentium 28). The priest can be described in four ways:

1 **a disciple**: someone who has heard Jesus' call to follow him
2 **an apostle**: in that he is sent out to serve others, concerned for all people, not just those in his parish
3 **a presbyter**: someone who has a duty to care for and support a group of people
4 **one who presides**: he leads, gathers them together for Mass and gives absolution.

A priest has certain duties to do with sacraments and certain pastoral duties.

The duties of a priest

Above all other things the priest is the **minister of the Eucharist**. Catholics believe that only a priest can consecrate the bread and the wine at Mass. This is the central part of the Mass, when Christ becomes present in the ceremony

Conducting funerals

Serving the wider world through charitable concerns and other activities

Proclaiming the Word: preaching and sharing God's message of love to help his people grow in faith

Visiting the sick and bereaved: remembering the importance of healing in Jesus' ministry, a priest visits members of the parish who are sick or suffering bereavement and may take communion to them. He may also offer them the Sacrament of the Sick

Offering absolution in the Sacrament of Reconciliation (Confession): only a priest has the power to offer absolution, which means confirming that the person really is forgiven by God

Leading the Christian community in worship

Leading the Parish council

Serving the wider world through charitable concerns and other activities

Christian initiation: baptising new members of the Church. He may prepare the parents of new babies who wish for baptism for the child, as well as adults who are interested in joining the Church. He prepares candidates for confirmation

A

Activities

1. Look at the duties of a priest in Diagram A. Construct an imaginary weekly diary of appointments with a range of different activities timetabled in. Think about including regular events, such as daily Mass, more masses on Sunday, perhaps also a special Holy Feast Day such as Good Friday, some time for confessions, some times for special groups that might meet, as well as particular events such as meeting a young couple thinking of getting married, counselling a member of the parish who is having difficulties, a special baptism. Think about whether certain activities need preparation time and also allow some time for your priest to have a day off and perhaps even some recreation!

2. Now look at the week you have prepared. What sorts of things might prove most challenging? Could there be any difficulties that the priest must overcome? Would he need to do any special preparation?

3. Having spent some time thinking about what a priest has to do, write in your own words what qualities you think a priest needs to have in order to serve God and his Church, and devise a 'recruitment' poster for the Church.

The importance and challenge of priesthood

- The priest works as part of a ministry team collaborating with deacons and lay people working together in the Church.

- The priest is a vital part of the life and service of the Catholic Church. If a man has received a special calling from God, and spent time finding out what he is being called to do, then he may choose to follow the priesthood of Christ.

- To be a priest is not to be someone who is better than other Christians. It is a particular role of service to which some are called and are able to perform the duties.

Activities

4. In what ways is a priest right at the centre of the most important periods of a person's life?

5. In what ways might it be important for a priest to be within the community?

6. In what ways might it be important for a priest to be apart from the community?

> 66 *Jesus is the priest, the teacher and the shepherd. [These] are the priorities for every bishop and for every priest. As priests, our first task and responsibility is to stand day by day at the altar and enable our parish communities to share in that greatest of all events which is the Sacrifice of the Mass.* 99
>
> Cardinal B. Hume, *To Be a Pilgrim*, SPCK, 1984

Extension activity

Ask a school chaplain or local priest to come and talk about their working week and what they would put on the 'recruitment poster'.

B   *A priest saying Mass*

∞ links

If you have not yet completed the extension activity on page 48, you could do so now.

AQA   Examiner's tip

Be sure you know the range of different roles of a priest, and are clear which are most important of all.

Summary

You should now understand that priests play vitally important roles in the life of the Parish. At the heart of the priest's role is celebration of Mass, but it extends into many other areas of care, teaching and support.

The Rite of Ordination

The ordination of priests

In the Roman Catholic Church, priests are ordained by the bishop after a long period of reflection, preparation and training. During that time they are taught about the different aspects of their role, but even more importantly, they listen to the calling they have received from God to be sure they should ask for **ordination**.

Activity

1. Photos **A**, **B**, and **C** reflect stages of the Rite of Ordination. What is going on in each of these photos?

A

B

C

D The order of service

Summary	Description	Explanation
Presentation	The candidate is called forward to be presented to the bishop.	
The Examination	The bishop questions the candidate about his responsibilities including obedience to the bishop and celebrating the sacraments. The candidate promises to fulfil them.	It is important that the candidate is willing to accept the duties and responsibilities of priesthood.
Prostration	The candidate lies on the floor in prostration.	This is a sign that he is submitting himself to God.
Consecration	The priest is ordained by the bishop, by laying on of hands and by prayer.	The laying on of hands is an ancient sign of the conferring of authority on someone. It is also a sign of the presence of the Holy Spirit. 'they prayed and laid their hands upon them' (Acts 6:1–6).
Prayer	The bishop gives a prayer of thanks to God.	The priesthood is a gift from God to his Church.
Investment	New priests are invested with the stole and chasuble.	These are the Eucharistic garments of office. They show that the wearer is a priest.
Anointing	The bishop anoints the priest's hands with oil.	As with Christ, the hands are anointed to bless, consecrate and sanctify.
Mass	The bishop presents him with the paten and chalice and the priest assists the bishop in celebrating Mass.	The paten and chalice are symbolic of the priest's duty as minister of the Eucharist which he then begins.

The examination of the candidates

During the rite of ordination, the candidate or candidates are asked questions and asked to make promises. Read the following extract from the rite:

Bishop: My sons, before you proceed to the order of the presbyterate, declare before the people your intention to undertake the office. Are you resolved, with the help of the Holy Spirit, to discharge without fail the office of the priesthood in the presbyteral order as a conscientious fellow worker with the bishops in caring for the Lord's flock?

Candidates: I am

Bishop: Are you resolved to celebrate the mysteries of Christ faithfully and religiously as the Church has handed them down to us for the glory of God and the sanctification of God's people?

Candidates: I am

Bishop: Are you resolved to exercise the ministry of the word worthily and wisely, preaching the Gospel and explaining the Catholic faith?

Candidates: I am

Bishop: Are you resolved to consecrate your life to God for the salvation of his people, and to unite yourself more closely to every day to Christ the High Priest, who offered himself for us to the Father as a perfect sacrifice?

Candidates: I am, with the help of God

Bishop: Do you promise respect and obedience to me and my successors?

Candidates: I do

Bishop: May God who has begun the good work in you bring it to fulfilment.

From: www.carr.org/~meripper/faith/o-priest.htm

Key terms

Ordination: the status of being ordained to a sacred office: a deacon, priest or bishop.

Activity

2   Create a poster or leaflet showing both the stages of the Rite of Ordination and also the meaning behind some of those stages.

Activities

3   What can you learn from the examination of the candidates about the role and duties of the priest?

4   Suggest three ways in which the Rite of Ordination is similar to the marriage rite.

5   How do the different actions in the Rite of Ordination show what it means to be a priest?

Summary

You should now know that priests are ordained by bishops. The Rite of Ordination is an important rite in the Roman Catholic Church.

AQA   Examiner's tip

There are many symbols in the Rite of Ordination. Make sure you know what these symbols mean.

3.7 Issues 1: celibacy

■ The importance of celibacy in Catholic priesthood

In the Roman Catholic Church, there is a long tradition that priests are **celibate**. This means they do not take a wife or partner and do not have sexual relations. The tradition of celibacy is suited to the priesthood in many ways:

- It is following the example of Christ, who did not marry.
- It is easier to remain focused on Christ and his Church with undivided love.
- Marriage and family life is demanding and time consuming. There must be no competition between the love of a wife and family, and the love of everyone in the parish.
- Priests often need to be moved to new situations and this would be difficult for someone with family commitments.

There is much debate about this issue, especially at a time when there is a shortage of priests in some parts of the Church. However, this is a rule that the Church has set.

> 66 Celibacy is one of the ways in which the priest takes on the undivided heart of Jesus himself. It is a challenge to love at the deepest level, a love without limits and open for all, a love which makes present the gentle power of the love of God. Celibacy is an opportunity to be really free in one's service of others. When lived in love for Jesus Christ, it gives the priest an inner freedom to cherish God's people with the love of the Good Shepherd. It leaves him totally open and available for those he serves and free to move to wherever he can best be of service. 99
>
> A Catholic Priest: Today and Tomorrow, Michael Evans, Committee for Ministerial Formation, Bishops' Conference of England and Wales, 1993, p28

Objectives

Explain the importance of celibacy for priesthood in the Catholic tradition.

Consider the arguments for and against a married priesthood.

Key terms

Celibacy: the obligation to abstain from sexual relationships; part of the vows taken by people entering religious life.

Extension activity

Read this quotation of Michael Evans again carefully and explain it in your own words.

Activities

1. What are the arguments that a priest should be celibate?
2. Which of these arguments do you find most persuasive and why?
3. Which of these arguments do you find least persuasive and why?

A Could you ever become a Catholic priest?

Married Catholic priests

There are a few married Catholic priests! Although celibacy is the norm for all priests who were Catholic when they chose to become priests, there are a few married priests in the Catholic Church who converted from the Church of England. Special permission was granted to make this possible as these men were married and ordained in a Church which allowed for a married priesthood.

B

■ Arguments for married Catholic priests

Within the Church of England, as well as other Protestant Churches, celibacy is not required. Within the Orthodox Church, celibacy is optional for priests. This has led to some argument about the possibility of permitting Catholic priests to marry. Arguments in favour of this include:

- The men Jesus chose to be his disciples were married, even though he was not. This includes St Peter (Jesus healed his mother-in-law, Matthew 8:14; Mark 1:30; Luke 4:38).

- A priest who experiences the challenge of family life may be better able to understand and support parishioners who are having family difficulties.

- Celibacy is not a normal situation for all men to be in and some men may be called both to priesthood and to marriage. These men currently cannot follow both vocations.

- Celibacy distances the priest from ordinary human life and so distances him from his parish community.

- There is a great shortage of priests in some parts of the Church. Allowing married priests might help this shortage.

Activities

4 Organise the arguments for married priests in order of how convincing you think the reasons are, from most convincing to least convincing.

5 Explain the reasons for your decisions about the list.

Discussion activity 👥

Hold a group or class discussion about the question 'Should the Catholic Church allow married priests?'

Summary

You should now understand that the Catholic Church teaches that ordinarily priests should be celibate. Some argue that priests should be allowed to marry.

AQA **Examiner's tip**

Make sure you understand why it is that celibacy is the norm for Catholic priests, even though there are some exceptions.

Issues 2: the ordination of women

The male priesthood

Women cannot be ordained in the Catholic Church. They share in the common priesthood that all lay people share in, but cannot become priests. The Catholic Church maintains a very strict teaching in this area. Any bishop who tries to ordain women and women who try to be ordained may both be excommunicated.

Objectives

Explain why the Catholic Churches teaches that priesthood is for men only.

Consider the arguments for and against women priests.

A   *Arguments for and against the ordination of women*

The Catholic Church's arguments against the ordination of women	Arguments for the ordination of women
There is a long standing tradition in both the western and eastern Church that only men can be ordained. How can the Church today break that tradition?	The Church has changed other long standing traditions. For instance until the 1960s the Sacrament of the Eucharist could only be said in Latin. Now it can be said in the local language.
Christ only appointed men as apostles.	The biblical evidence is not conclusive. There are some references to women having leading responsibility in the New Testament and in the early Church (See Romans 16:7 for instance). Moreover, women's position in society was very different in the time of Jesus to what it is today.
There are other ways women may serve God in lay life or by taking religious orders.	Some women feel they are called to be priests. If God is calling them, then the Church should allow them to answer that call.
The priest in the liturgy presides as a symbol of Christ (in persona Christi), the bridegroom of the Church (Ephesians 5.29–32) and there should be some similarity between the priest and Christ (he should be male).	If God made everyone in his image (as stated in Genesis) then surely any human being can represent Christ at the altar?

B   *Jesus at the Last Supper surrounded by his male apostles*

Women ministers in other churches

Women are ordained in other churches. A number of nonconformist churches have had women ministers for many years, though they do not all see a minister as a priest in the way the Catholic Church does. For instance a woman minister does not represent Christ at the altar during communion services in the United Reformed Church. The Church of England has ordained women as priests for some years and in some parts of the Anglican Communion there are women bishops although this has caused arguments within the Anglican Church.

C *This photograph is of a 9th-century mosaic in the Church of St Praxedis in Rome. The Virgin Mary is in the blue mantle. On her left is St Pudentiana and on her right St Praxedis. They are believed to have been leaders of house churches in early Christian Rome. Episcopa Theodora is argued by some to have been the bishop of the Church of St Praxedis in 820 AD, but she may have been the wife of the Bishop*

Activity

Consider all the arguments for and against women priests. Identify the stronger and weaker arguments for each view and give reasons for your choices. Then decide for yourself what you think, using the arguments to inform your answer.

AQA Examiner's tip

Link the arguments about women priests to the actions of Christ and the early Church.

Summary

You should now know that the Catholic Church teaches that only men can become priests. Some are in favour of women priests or ministers.

Vocation and the religious life

All Christians are called to give their lives as a witness to Christ. So far in this chapter we have looked at how people may be called to serve God and the Church as a lay person and how some are called to be deacons or priests to serve in Holy Orders. However some are called to consecrate their lives to Christ. This means they promise to give their life in the service of God.

> 66 Men Wanted for hazardous journey. Small wages, bitter cold, long months of complete darkness, constant danger, safe return doubtful, honour and recognition in case of success. 99
>
> Ernest Shackleton, Antarctic Explorer, 1914. 5000 applicants apparently

> 66 Men Wanted, to discover where God may be calling them. Exciting journey, challenging year, safe return probable but with new personal insights. No wages but honour and recognition in high places. 99
>
> From www.augustinians.org.uk/

What is the religious life?

The **religious life** is a calling to live like Jesus in **poverty**, **chastity** and **obedience**. It is the dedication of oneself to God through serving the Church and working for the salvation of the world.

There are many different ways in which people can consecrate their lives to Christ. In 1 Corinthians 12:4–7, St Paul writes of the many different gifts that come from the same spirit. The Catholic Church teaches that God calls everyone and has a specific and different purpose for everyone in his plan. Being called by God is part of being human.

Religious sisters, brothers and priests

Men and women can choose to live the religious life. They pronounce publicly vows of poverty, chastity and obedience. They then live in a community and share a common life. These men and women are called 'the religious'. Women are called 'sisters' and men are called 'brothers'. If men choose to live a consecrated life and have been ordained, their title is 'father'. Religious life takes two main forms: apostolic (active) orders and contemplative orders.

∞ links

For definitions and more about apostolic and contemplative orders, see the following pages 60–61.

For definitions and more about apostolic and contemplative orders, see the following pages 60–61.

Objectives

Know and understand what is meant by a vocation to the religious life.

Explain what is mean by poverty, chastity and obedience and why they are important vows for the religious life.

Key terms

Religious life: dedicating life to God, taking vows and living in a particular holy way.

Poverty: living simply and sharing talents, money, and material goods for the support of the community.

Chastity: making a vow not to take a wife, husband or partner and not to have sexual relations.

Obedience: obeying the superior (person in charge) of the religious order.

A   *Those who choose the religious life choose to live like Jesus in poverty, chastity and obedience*

What do the vows mean?

B

Vow of poverty	The vow of poverty means living simply and sharing talents, money, and material goods for the support of the community. The Acts of the Apostles records how the early Church shared their possessions.
Vow of chastity	The vow of chastity is also known as celibacy. It means choosing to share love and friendship with all of God's people, rather than making a commitment to a single person in marriage. It is the promise to love all and serve all as completely as possible. Jesus chose no wife but gave his life for his father and his love for all.
Vow of obedience	The vow of obedience means obeying the superior in the order. The religious must listen to and obey God's will as it is understood through prayer and also their order. Jesus obeyed the will of his father, even in ultimately accepting his duty to sacrifice himself. 'Father, not my will but yours' were the words he spoke in the Garden of Gethsemane before his crucifixion.

Extension activity

1 Read Acts 4:32–35. How can this be linked to one of the vows?

AQA Examiner's tip

Learn definitions of the vows of poverty, chastity and obedience.

Activities

1. Explain how the vows help to sustain and maintain the consecrated life?
2. Why do you think having married monks and nuns might prove very difficult?
3. Common sense suggests that getting on in life is about freedom to do what we like, succeeding in life, and having financial rewards. How does the idea of Christian vocation to religious life turn that idea upside down? Why do you think that so many people choose that road in life?
4. What questions would you ask someone thinking about taking vows of poverty, chastity and obedience? What answers might they give?

Extension activity

2 You can explore Activity 4 in roleplay.

Scene 1

Partner A plays the person who wants to pursue religious life. Partner B is a sceptical friend. B asks A three questions which A has to answer. In preparation A and B should think about these questions and try to develop an interesting angle in the exchange. Perhaps A has not thought things through. This may come out in the questioning. Perhaps it is B who has got things wrong.

Scene 2

Partner B plays the person who wants to pursue religious life and Partner A plays the Superior of the Order questioning the new applicant. Again, plan for three questions and answers. Think through what you might want to show from the scene. What sort of thing do you think a Superior might be looking for in the answers a person gives?

Summary

You should now understand that a vocation to the religious life is a calling to consecrate one's life to Christ. This involves taking vows of poverty, chastity and obedience in a contemplative or apostolic order.

3.10 Examples of religious life

Different ways of responding to the Christian vocation in the religious life

St Paul teaches that the Holy Spirit gives many different gifts. He states that there are many different kinds of service and working, but the same Lord and the same God in all of them. There are many different religious orders, congregations, and societies offering different routes for those wishing to follow God's call.

Beliefs and teachings

There are different kinds of gifts, but the same Spirit. There are different kinds of service, but the same Lord. There are different kinds of working, but the same God works all of them in all men.

1 Corinthians 12:4-6

What is the difference between apostolic and contemplative religious life?

There are many different groups of religious orders living out their vocation. Some, such as the Carthusians, are exclusively **contemplative**, living in enclosed communities and centring their life around prayer. Others such as the Society of Jesus (Jesuits) are exclusively **apostolic**, working out in the world. Others, such as the Carmelites, are divided into different communities, some of an apostolic nature, others of a contemplative nature.

Those in religious orders may have traditional clothes, such as a habit, or may dress in ordinary clothes.

Objectives

Explore what Christians believe about how the different gifts of the spirit, different kinds of service and work may reflect Christian vocation.

Examine the difference between apostolic and contemplative religious life.

Analyse how particular religious communities live out a Christian vocation.

Key terms

Contemplative: in the context of Christian Vocation, this applies to those who choose to live out their vocation in structured prayer, meditation and work, usually in enclosed religious orders.

Apostolic: religious communities which combine a life of prayer with a life working in the world, for example in education.

A

Contemplative religious life	Apostolic religious life
■ Centred around prayer. These monks and nuns live separate lives from the world so that they may focus their prayers on the needs of the Church and the world. ■ They may stay within the community house, or they may be semi-contemplative (undertaking some part time work). ■ They also undertake work in agriculture or making liturgical items for the Church and so on.	■ Apostolic orders have a life of prayer. ■ They are actively involved outside their monastery, convent or house. ■ They are involved in different works of the Church: education, health care, serving the poor, assisting parishes or other Church organisations.

B *Clothing for a Jesuit religious*

C *Clothing for a Chartreux religious*

D *Clothing for a Carmelite religious*

Activities

After studying Table **E**, answer these questions.

1 What are the differences between apostolic and contemplative approaches to religious life?

2 'I can understand the point of apostolic religious life, but what is the use of contemplatives?' Suggest why someone might express this view and then give reasons against it.

3 Give three examples of the kind of work that members of religious orders might do.

4 Explain how this work is connected to the mission and spirituality of the Order.

E Different religious communities have distinctive histories, spiritualities and missions.

Community	History	Spirituality	Mission
The Society of Jesus – also known as the Jesuits (Extracted from the Jesuits in Britain website www.jesuit. org.uk)	A religious order of men, within the Catholic Church. Founded in 1540 by Ignatius of Loyola and nine companions, the Society now numbers twenty thousand men and is present in more than 100 countries.	'The loving God is very active in our lives, seeking to heal us and bring us closer. He encourages us to enter the gospel scenes with the help of our imaginations and thus get to know Jesus personally as a friend whom we can trust and say anything to.'	Jesuits take vows of poverty, chastity and obedience, and live together in a community. They are engaged in a wide variety of works: there are Jesuit parish priests, spiritual directors, writers and teachers, but also actors, lawyers, doctors, sculptors and astronomers.
Carmelites (Extracts from www. carmelite.org/ and www.carmelites.com/)	The First Order is the friars (who are active/contemplative), the Second Order is the nuns (who are cloistered). From the small group of perhaps 20 or 30 men who left the slopes of Carmel at the beginning of the 13th century there are today some 2,000 friars, 920 cloistered nuns and 3,200 active sisters.	'Carmel stands for the intimate encounter which God brings about between the person and God in the midst of all that is most ordinary in life. So, if you are seeking visions and ecstatic experiences then you are in the wrong place. This is the mystery of the "Word made flesh" who "emptied himself to take the form of a slave ... and then was humbler still ..."'	The primary mission is to follow Jesus Christ through prayer, fraternity, and prophetic service in the presence of the spirit of Mary and Elijah. Their chief means for fulfilling this mission is by their lives and ministries. They work to develop and encourage a sense of contemplative service to all God's people, with special attention to the poor and to developing lay participation in the Church.
Carthusians (Extracts from the Carthusians website www.chartreux.org/ en/frame.html)	The Order was founded by Saint Bruno in 1084 and comprises a masculine and a feminine branch. At present, the Order is composed of about 450 monks and nuns who live a solitary life at the heart of the Church; there are 24 Houses in three continents, all dedicated exclusively to the contemplative life.	'Our principal endeavour and goal is to devote ourselves to the silence and solitude of cell ... There is the faithful soul frequently united with the Word of God; there is the bride made one with her spouse; there is earth joined to heaven, the divine to the human.' Statutes 4.1	The Carthusians consecrate their lives entirely to prayer and seeking God in the secret of their hearts. They intercede for the Church and for the salvation of the whole world. Their life finds its balance around: silence, solitude, living in cell; prayer in common in the church, three times a day, as well as some fraternal meetings; their own liturgy, adapted to their style of life and the small number of religious.

Summary

You should now understand that there are many different ways in which different orders, societies and congregations respond to God's call, but the people within them are united by a desire to dedicate their lives to serving God and his Church.

AQA Examiner's tip

While you do not need to learn these particular orders, they will help you understand different ways of living a religious life.

3

Christian vocation – summary

For the examination you should now be able to:

✔ explain the terms vocation, laity, priesthood, ordination, holy orders, deacon, celibacy, religious life, apostolic and contemplative

✔ explain the different ways Christians may respond to a Christian calling

✔ outline the different roles of lay people and priests in the Catholic Church

✔ outline the development of the priesthood

✔ explain the nature of holy orders

✔ explain the vows of poverty, chastity and obedience

✔ outline the ways in which religious orders fulfil the vocation of the religious

✔ explain the work of a deacon and the duties of a priest

✔ outline the service of ordination and the symbolic meaning of different parts of the service

✔ explain how important vocation is for the Christian life

✔ provide arguments to support Catholic teaching that priests should be celibate and the arguments against this view

✔ provide arguments to support Catholic teaching that women cannot be ordained and the arguments against this view.

Sample answer

1   Write an answer to the following exam question.

Explain the meaning and importance of the religious life in the Roman Catholic Church. *(6 marks)*

2   Read the following sample answer:

> Catholics believe that God calls them all to follow his teachings. Some feel that God wants them to serve him by being a monk or a nun. This means they promise not to have sex with others and to live a poor simple life. Some monks and nuns stay in their monasteries praying while others do things with people like teaching.

3   With a partner, discuss the sample answer. Do you think that there are other things that the student could have included in the answer?

4   What mark would you give this answer out of 6? Look at the mark scheme in the Introduction on page 7 (AO1). What are the reasons for the mark you have given?

AQA Examination-style questions

1 Look at the illustration and answer the following questions.

(a) What is meant by the word vocation? (*2 marks*)

(b) Explain the roles of the Roman Catholic priest. (*6 marks*)

(c) Explain why the Roman Catholic Church is opposed to women's ordination. (*4 marks*)

(d) 'Priests should remain celibate!'
    Do you agree? Give reasons for your answer, showing that you have thought about more than one point of view. Refer to Roman Catholic teaching in your answer. (*6 marks*)

Examiner's tip When referring to Roman Catholic teaching you can use Bible references and teachings of the Church. Try to explain these teachings when you use them in your answer.

4.1 Sin in the Roman Catholic tradition

■ Sin

Sin can be described in many ways. It:

- is a barrier preventing people from being close to God in their life
- is turning away from the ways of Jesus
- is not living by God's law, the beatitudes and the commandments
- includes both things that we may do and things that we may allow to happen, that we do not prevent (a sin of omission)
- may be a deliberate choice, or something we are too weak to resist doing.

Original sin

The Catholic Church teaches that human beings are flawed. Something about the nature of humans means they are drawn to doing evil. This is passed down from generation to generation beginning with the first sin of Adam and Eve (eating fruit of the tree of the knowledge of good and evil). All people are born into a sinful world and this original sin means that people tend to sin. However, human beings are able to tell the difference between right and wrong so can resist evil and can do good instead.

Key terms

Sin: behaviour which is against God's laws and wishes and against principles of morality. A thought or action which is wrong, we know is wrong and we freely choose.

Venial and mortal sins

Sin is not simply a mistake or doing something badly. Catholic teaching divides sin into venial sins and mortal sins. Venial sins are not grave, not committed with full knowledge and not entirely deliberate, whilst mortal sin is a very grave sin committed deliberately with full knowledge. Mortal sins are so grave that a person is in a serious state of needing forgiveness and salvation.

Activity

1 Suggest an action that would fit the following categories. Then identify whether each of the actions you choose could be a deliberate choice, or could be something that the person was too weak to resist doing.

a rejecting God's commandments and Beatitudes

b failing to follow Christ's actions.

> 66 *We sin from frailty and from malice. There are of course those sins of weakness when we are overcome by passion and by our weakness. There are those calculated and deliberate decisions to do what is wrong for the sake of our own advantage or self-interest. But in some measure, all of us are burdened with sin.* 99
>
> Cardinal Basil Hume

Activity

2 Suggest examples of sins which could be considered venial and sins which could be considered mortal. Use the definitions in the text to explore these suggestions and decide what you think about any sins that could be either venial or mortal.

Sorrow and guilt

Sorrow is a natural response to sin. The Catholic Church teaches that sorrow is an important first step because it is a sign that a person has recognised that they have done wrong and genuinely want things to be different. Many people feel guilt in their lives for all sorts of reasons, such as:

- regrets about things they wish they had done differently
- an inability to see anything good about themselves
- a sense from others that they are failures and have not lived up to expectations or have made the wrong choices.

Although Christian conscience plays an important role in guiding a person about their moral actions, an over-bearing sense of guilt can make it impossible for someone to follow God's law of love, loving others as they love themselves. This in turn can lead to:

- anxiety and depression
- a sense of spiritual isolation and drifting away from the Church and their faith.

Guilt can bear down on people so they are unable to realise both God's love of them and his desire that they should return to him.

A   *People can feel imprisoned by a sense of guilt and feel apart from God and the Church*

A world in need of reconciliation

There is much conflict in the world because of sin: wars, divisions in families or between groups in society, breakdown between the young and the old and religious disputes to name but a few. For Christians this means there is a real need for healing, peace and **reconciliation**. This can be broken down into four parts:

- **Reconciliation with yourself** (All people are made in God's image and likeness and have the capacity to be like Christ).
- **Reconciliation with others** (God commends everyone to love each other).
- **Reconciliation with the Church** (God wants the human family to be united, one in his Spirit).
- **Reconciliation with God** (God wants people to return to him because he loves them).

Key terms

Reconciliation: a sacrament in the Roman Catholic Church; when two people or groups of people who have disagreed or fought with each other make up.

Extension activity

Look at a newspaper or news website. Find stories which show a need for reconciliation.

Activities

3   Why might someone come to dislike themselves or feel they are worthless?

4   Suggest five different ways in which people are divided or harmed by sin? Give examples of being divided from God, the Church and their neighbour.

AQA   *Examiner's tip*

Remember that reconciliation is not just about forgiving a person who has done wrong, but includes healing divisions between people and God and the Church.

Summary

You should now know that the Church teaches that the world is separated from God and in need of reconciliation.

4.2 Forgiveness in the Roman Catholic tradition

Reconciliation and redeeming love

The Bible provides many examples of teachings and stories which show that God's love is a forgiving love and a saving love. It saves people from their sin. Some feel that they are unlovable, or that they cannot be reached by God's forgiveness. The Bible teaches that God wants to reconcile human beings with him.

Beliefs and teachings

God redeems your life from the pit.

Psalms 103:4

You will cast all our sins into the depths of the sea.

Micah 7:19

In the New Testament

When Jesus met people whom others called sinners, he did not react with blame, anger, or criticism. He welcomed them, sat and ate with them, offered them friendship and forgiveness. When Jesus showed people love, they were reconciled to God. He showed a redeeming love.

- When speaking before a crowd who were about to stone an adulterous woman, he said to her 'neither do I condemn you' (see John 8:3–11).
- Shortly after this Jesus said, 'I did not come to judge the world, but to save it' (John 12:47).

The Sacrament of Reconciliation is based on these teachings. It offers people a chance to start again on the pathway to God. For many Christians, the knowledge and reassurance that God is a God of loving forgiveness, is one of the reasons they ask for forgiveness.

Beliefs and teachings

Forgiveness of sins brings reconciliation with God, but also with the Church.

Catechism 1462

The need to forgive

When Christians pray using the Lord's Prayer, there is a line 'forgive us our sins as we forgive those who trespass against us'. That line expresses a desire to be forgiven by God, but also suggests that forgiveness is something that human beings must offer one another. If reconciliation is refused then divisions can never be healed.

Activity

1 Why do you think the vision of a forgiving God is so important for Christians?

Objectives

Know and understand New and Old Testament teachings about God's forgiving and redeeming love.

Understand different interpretations of the parable of the Unmerciful Servant.

Key terms

Unmerciful: not showing forgiveness.

A God's love is a redeeming love that offers new life

The Unmerciful Servant

Therefore, the kingdom of heaven is like a king who wanted to settle accounts with his servants. As he began the settlement, a man who owed him ten thousand talents was brought to him. Since he was not able to pay, the master ordered that he and his wife and his children and all that he had be sold to repay the debt. The servant fell on his knees before him. 'Be patient with me,' he begged, 'and I will pay back everything.' The servant's master took pity on him, cancelled the debt and let him go. But when that servant went out, he found one of his fellow-servants who owed him a hundred denarii. He grabbed him and began to choke him. 'Pay back what you owe me!' he demanded.

His fellow-servant fell to his knees and begged him, 'Be patient with me, and I will pay you back.' But he refused. Instead, he went off and had the man thrown into prison until he could pay the debt. When the other servants saw what had happened, they were greatly distressed and went and told their master everything that had happened. Then the master called the servant in. 'You wicked servant,' he said, 'I cancelled all that debt of yours because you begged me to. Shouldn't you have had mercy on your fellow-servant just as I had on you?' In anger his master turned him over to the jailers to be tortured, until he should pay back all he owed. This is how my heavenly Father will treat each of you unless you forgive your brother from your heart.

Matthew 18:23–35

Interpreting the text

There are a number of ways in which this text may be interpreted:

- God's divine mercy and forgiveness should not be abused by failing to show mercy and forgiveness to others.
- Christians believe that they must forgive those who have sinned against them if they are to receive God's forgiveness themselves – those who do not forgive are punished.
- To be able to receive forgiveness, one must have a heart that forgives others.
- Christians must try to be Godlike in their forgiveness of others.

Forgiveness is by no means easy. The Church teaches that it is not human power which gives us the capacity to forgive but by turning one's heart to God. He can transform the pain and the misery of past sins.

Activities

2 In groups, suggest nine different things that a person can do as a sin against a neighbour and/or a sin against God (you could use the first section of the book or come up with your own ideas). Try to arrange them in order of how difficult they are to forgive, with the most difficult to forgive at the top.

3 Look at the different interpretations offered for the Parable of the Unmerciful Servant. Which do you think more closely fits the story? Give reasons for your answer.

4 Why is forgiveness sometimes so difficult to do? Think of a particular example when writing your answer.

Summary

You show now know that the New and Old Testaments teach about God's forgiving and redeeming love. The Parable of the Unmerciful Servant is a reminder that Christians should forgive others just as they ask God for forgiveness.

4.3 The rite and symbolism of reconciliation

Background

The Church teaches that the Sacrament of Reconciliation was instituted by Jesus when he showed himself to his Apostles after he had risen from the dead and said, 'receive the Holy Spirit. If you forgive anyone his sins, they are forgiven; if you do not forgive them, they are not forgiven.' (John 20:22–23). The sacrament has been known as many things, including **confession** and **penance**. Traditionally the sacrament took place in a confessional, a small enclosed box in which a person confessed their sins privately to a priest, expressed their **contrition** and gave an undertaking to try not to sin again.

Objectives

Know and understand the differences between individual and communal reconciliation.

Understand and be able to explain the different aspects of the Rite of Reconciliation.

Beliefs and teachings

Jesus insists on conversion of heart: reconciliation with one's brother before presenting an offering on the altar, love of enemies, and prayer for persecutors, prayer to the Father in secret, not heaping up empty phrases, prayerful forgiveness from the depths of the heart, purity of heart, and seeking the Kingdom before all else.

Catechism 2608

Key terms

Confession: acknowledging and stating sins committed.

Penance: an act, such as prayer, required of a person who has received God's forgiveness.

Contrition: a genuine sense of being sorry for sins committed.

Absolution: the removal of the guilt that results from sin; the final part of the sacrament of reconciliation; forgiveness.

Individual reconciliation/confession

This is the closest expression of a personal encounter with God and includes **absolution**. It is a private opportunity to speak to a priest, show contrition (that is, sorrow for sin) and hear the words of God's forgiveness personally.

A *What happens during individual confession?*

The action	Meanings and effects
Preparation	Reading scripture and silent prayer.
The sign of the cross and blessing	Focuses on the love of God.
Confession 'Bless me father for I have sinned …'	A person examines their conscience with respect to the commandments and the beatitudes. In actually confessing sins a person accepts responsibility for their actions or inactions.
Satisfaction/Penance	There may be some conversation between the priest and the person confessing to help explore the issues. The priest may give a penance, a requirement to do something such as further prayer.
Contrition 'Oh My God, I am very sorry that I have sinned against you. Because you are so good, and with your help, I will try not to sin again. Amen' (A simple form of the prayer the penitent says)	This means being genuinely sorry for ones own sins, and being determined to try not to sin again – a change of heart, a decision to try and be different in future, with God's help. The motivation for contrition should be a desire for the love of God, but it may come from a fear of God's punishment.
Absolution	The priest gives the prayer of absolution 'and I absolve you from your sins'. In Matthew 16:19, Jesus said to his Apostles 'whatever you bind on earth will be bound in heaven' and in so doing gave authority to bishops and priests to claim that God has forgiven the sinner.

Communal reconciliation/confession

These acts of worship bring out the social aspect of reconciliation. They allow the members of the same community to prepare together for festivals such as Christmas and Easter. They emphasise that reconciliation can take time and may lead to individual reconciliation. On special occasions these services may include a communal absolution. However, individual confession may also be available during the service.

B *What happens during communal confession?*

The actions	Meanings and effects
■ Begins with a hymn and opening prayer ■ Liturgy of the Word ■ Examination of conscience (how well a person is living by the commandments and beatitudes) ■ Individual reconciliation/confession ■ Absolution ■ Prayers of praise and thanksgiving and final blessing	■ Confession takes place in prayer and the liturgy of the word. ■ The community joins together to prepare for individual confession. ■ Helps the person remember that sin affects God and others ■ The examination of conscience together helps individuals to have a sense of the body of Christ in the community.

C *This shows a newer style of confessional which can be in secret or face to face*

Absolution

To be absolved from sin means to be clear from any guilt or blame. It means to forgive and to forget. It is to wipe clean the slate, to offer new life to the person.

Beliefs and teachings

God, the Father of mercies, through the death and resurrection of his Son has reconciled the world to himself and sent the Holy Spirit among us for the forgiveness of sins; through the ministry of the church may God give you pardon and peace, and I absolve you from your sins in the name of the Father, and of the Son, and of the Holy Spirit. ([The person confessing] answers:) Amen.

From the new Rite of Penance, 1974

The prayer of absolution emphasises important Christian beliefs: that Jesus reconciled human beings to God through his death and resurrection, that he sent his Spirit for the forgiveness of sins, and that he gave to his priests and bishops authority to pronounce God's forgiveness.

D *Misconceptions about absolution*

Misconceptions	Actual beliefs based on the Church's teachings
'It is an opportunity to be told off for what you have done wrong!'	The sacrament is an opportunity to ask for and receive forgiveness for your sins.
'You just have to say the words and you will be forgiven! It is a let off!'	You must be genuinely contrite (genuinely sorry and with a genuine desire for change).
'Your sins are much worse than anyone else's. God cannot forgive you!'	No one is beyond the possibility of God's forgiveness.
'The Priest cannot be trusted with your secrets!'	Priests are bound to never reveal the conversations from the Sacrament of Reconciliation in any way.

Activities

1 Identify how each part of the Prayer of Absolution relates to a key Christian belief.

2 What are the different advantages of individual and communal reconciliation?

AQA *Examiner's tip*

Make sure you understand how absolution is linked to Christian beliefs about God's forgiveness.

Summary

You should now understand that the Sacrament of Reconciliation mainly involves confession of sins and an act of contrition and absolution, which involves total loving forgiveness.

The importance of the Sacrament of Reconciliation

A *Reasons why some people avoid the sacrament*

Reason	Explanation
Fear and anxiety	For many people the Sacrament of Reconciliation is something they fear or are very anxious about. People are uncertain about what they should do – do they list their sins? Will the priest be understanding? Will it be embarrassing?
Guilt	They may fear they are too far gone or beyond the possibility of forgiveness.
Misunderstanding	They may feel they have not done anything wrong enough in their lives and do not need forgiveness.

■ The effects of the Sacrament of Reconciliation

The Catholic Church teaches that the sacrament offers many things, in particular:

- reconciliation with God by which the penitent recovers grace (undeserved favour with God which is freely given)
- reconciliation with the Church
- release from the eternal punishment incurred by mortal sins
- release at least in part from time in purgatory (a place of purification of sin for a person who has died, which brings them closer to God in Heaven)
- peace and serenity of conscience
- an increase of spiritual strength against evil.

The sacrament is a way in which healing can come to an individual person, and to the Christian community as a whole.

∞ links

To find out more about purgatory, see pages 96–97.

Activity

1 Explain the different kinds of healing that the sacrament offers. Use the effects of the sacrament to help with your answer.

■ God has made the first move

One of the reasons for the change from the word 'confession' to 'reconciliation' is that reconciliation more accurately reflects the Christian belief that God has already set out to find his lost sheep (those who have sinned). He has already begun on the path towards forgiveness. The word 'confession' captures only the human action towards God but the word 'reconciliation' includes God's commitment to his people.

Objectives

Understand why some people may not go to receive the sacrament.

Know and understand the different effects and impact of the Sacrament of Reconciliation.

Analyse the Parable of the Forgiving Father and understand how it is connected with Christian beliefs about the Sacrament of Reconciliation.

❝ *Many people who come to the sacrament come with immense anxieties ... They feel on the margin. ... The Sacrament of Reconciliation must be an opportunity for creative encounter and healing help.* ❞

Father Wilfred McGreal

Beliefs and teachings

If we claim we are without sin, we deceive ourselves and the truth is not in us

1 John 1:8

I will forgive their wickedness, and remember their sins no more.

Jeremiah 31:34

Beliefs and teachings

The Parable of the Forgiving Father
(sometimes referred to as the Lost Son or the Prodigal Son)

Jesus continued: There was a man who had two sons. The younger one said to his father, 'Father, give me my share of the estate.' So he divided his property between them. Not long after that, the younger son got together all he had, set off for a distant country and there squandered his wealth in wild living. After he had spent everything, there was a severe famine in that whole country, and he began to be in need. So he went and hired himself out to a citizen of that country, who sent him to his fields to feed pigs. He longed to fill his stomach with the pods that the pigs were eating, but no-one gave him anything. When he came to his senses, he said, 'How many of my father's hired men have food to spare, and here I am starving to death! I will set out and go back to my father and say to him: Father, I have sinned against heaven and against you. I am no longer worthy to be called your son; make me like one of your hired men.'

So he got up and went to his father. But while he was still a long way off, his father saw him and was filled with compassion for him; he ran to his son, threw his arms around him and kissed him. The son said to him, 'Father, I have sinned against heaven and against you. I am no longer worthy to be called your son.' But the father said to his servants, 'Quick! Bring the best robe and put it on him. Put a ring on his finger and sandals on his feet. Bring the fattened calf and kill it. Let's have a feast and celebrate. For this son of mine was dead and is alive again; he was lost and is found.' So they began to celebrate.

Meanwhile, the older son was in the field. When he came near the house, he heard music and dancing. So he called one of the servants and asked him what was going on. 'Your brother has come,' he replied, 'and your father has killed the fattened calf because he has him back safe and sound.' The older brother became angry and refused to go in. So his father went out and pleaded with him. But he answered his father, 'Look! All these years I've been slaving for you and never disobeyed your orders. Yet you never gave me even a young goat so I could celebrate with my friends. But when this son of yours who has squandered your property with prostitutes comes home, you kill the fattened calf for him!' 'My son,' the father said, 'you are always with me, and everything I have is yours. But we had to celebrate and be glad, because this brother of yours was dead and is alive again; he was lost and is found.'

Luke 15:11–32

■ Interpreting the parable

There are many different ways of interpreting this parable which is traditionally understood to throw light on the relationship between God and human beings. Here are some of messages from it:

- The father has already begun to move towards reconciliation with the younger son even before the son openly confessed his sins. This shows the father's loving forgiveness. The son had an inner change of heart – he realised he has done wrong and set his heart on a new road, back to his father.

- The father acts as if the sins have never happened. He completely restores him to new life and begins a hero's return celebration, which baffles the other son.

- The elder son has to recognise that forgiveness is not something which must be earned or deserved and that all are entitled to receive the love of the Father.

AQA   *Examiner's tip*

Remember that it is not enough just to know the parable, you need to able to explain what it means to Christians.

Activities

2   Look back to the outline of the individual confession on page 68, Table **A**. Identify the following features in the parable: examining conscience, confessing sins, absolution.

3   How does the parable illustrate that reconciliation is a process that may take time?

4   In what ways might the father's reaction on seeing his lost son again throw light on Christian beliefs about God's forgiveness?

5   Why do you think the father's response does not seem to make sense to the other brother? Try to explain his reaction.

Summary

You should now know that the Church teaches that the Sacrament of Reconciliation offers people a chance to be reconciled to themselves, to others, to the Church and to God, and gives them peace and new life.

4.5 Causes of crime

What is crime?

Crime is not obeying a law established by a government, for which there is a punishment. Crime includes: violence, burglary, vandalism, theft, sexual offences, drug offences, fraud, forgery and criminal damage.

What are the causes of crime?

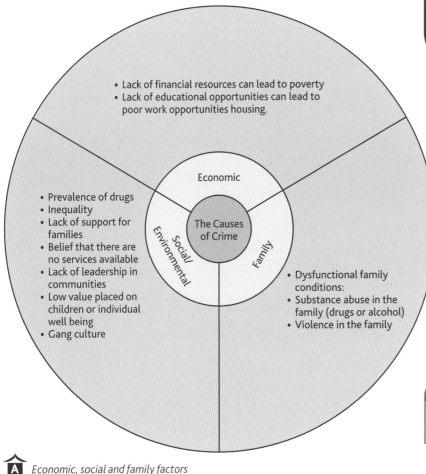

- Lack of financial resources can lead to poverty
- Lack of educational opportunities can lead to poor work opportunities housing.

Economic

The Causes of Crime

Social/Environmental

Family

- Prevalence of drugs
- Inequality
- Lack of support for families
- Belief that there are no services available
- Lack of leadership in communities
- Low value placed on children or individual well being
- Gang culture

- Dysfunctional family conditions:
- Substance abuse in the family (drugs or alcohol)
- Violence in the family

A *Economic, social and family factors*

Activity

1 'These causes (see Diagram **A**) are wrong! Not all poor people are criminals. Not all children from difficult family situations are criminals. Everyone has a choice and sometimes people make the wrong choice and we should not make excuses for them.'

To what extent do you think this is true? Give reason for your view.

Activity

2 Is a crime involving violence against a person more serious than a crime which takes resources away from public services, such as theft of medicines from a hospital? Give reasons for you answer.

Christian perspectives on the causes of crime

In addition, Christians might suggest these other causes:

- Moral failings: because Christians believe that as part of original sin, human beings are flawed and are more likely to be sinful. For instance, selfishness and greed can lead to crimes fuelled by desire.
- Evil or the devil: some Christians believe that the Devil or Satan may be actively causing crime by tempting people.

■ What impact does crime have on society?

The effects of crime

Crime has short and long term effects. It can cause the death or injury of a person or their loved ones. This may lead to loss of income and medical costs. Crime causes the costs of replacing stolen goods as well as security costs. Crime can leave the victim experiencing anxiety, depression or stress which can affect friends and can disrupt family life. Society can suffer from a fear of crime and be unable to enjoy life.

■ What is Catholic teaching about crime?

The Beatitudes and the commandments emphasise fairness, honesty, and justice. They suggest we must:

- live a life based on love of neighbour and love of God, not pursing one's own selfish interests
- not take or covet what is not yours ('Do not steal', 'do not covet')
- be honest in your dealings – do not lie ('Do not bear false witness')
- be an upholder of justice ('Blessed are those who hunger for righteousness', 'Blessed are the pure in heart')
- respect the value of human life ('Do not kill', 'Blessed are the peacemakers').

Christianity does not tolerate crimes which undermine family life and encourage selfishness.

■ When might Christians challenge the law?

Protest against the law

The story of Jesus turning over the moneychangers' tables at the Temple inspires some Christians to take things into their own hands. The teacher of the Church, St Thomas Aquinas, once said that a law that is an unjust law is no law at all. He thought that a law that encouraged immoral activity should not be followed. A Christian's duty to bring about a just world means they have to act against injustice.

A Christian might feel a moral dilemma in some situations. For instance, might it be justified to steal if you are starving? Should you pay taxes to your government if they are doing things you consider immoral?

Summary

You should now understand that crime goes against Christian values, although there may be situations when a civil law is against Christian teaching and when Christians might justify breaking the law.

Activities

3 Why do you think there is so much crime in society?

4 There are many crimes committed by young people against young people. Why do you think this is and what are the effects of such crimes?

5 Which of these do you think is the most damaging aspect of crime? Choose three and give reason for your choices.

Discussion activities

1 A rich tourist is walking through a market on holiday in a desperately poor country. He has a $10 dollar bill sticking out of his pocket, 2 months wages in this country. A boy from a family on the edge of starvation and sickness, sees the note and picks the man's pocket. He buys food and medicines for his family. Identify the Christian arguments for and against the boy's action. Decide which argument is stronger, on Christian grounds.

2 The law requires that people pay taxes of different kinds. These taxes are used to fund health services including abortion facilities. Could a Christian who believes that abortion is wrong and against God's law, be justified in refusing to pay taxes?

AQA Examiner's tip

Make sure you are able to explain several different causes of crime.

4.6 The aims of punishment

Why does society punish people?

There are four classic aims for punishment. These are covered in Table **A**.

A *Why does society punish people?*	
Retribution	This means revenge or repayment for what has been done against the laws of society or the individual.
	Some countries punish through physical beatings, and even the death penalty, out of retribution.
Deterrence	As a warning to others to try to discourage them from committing similar crimes, for example a person who has drawn on a wall with graffiti might be punished by having them clean the wall in public. Other people who see the criminal working will hopefully be put off from drawing graffiti because they don't want to have to clean it up.
Protection	Protecting society by stopping the individual criminals from being able to commit crimes against people, typically through prison, or some other restriction on a person's movement such as electronic tagging.
	This is especially important for those who threaten to harm individuals, undermining a sense of well-being and security.
Reform	To try to change the offender's behaviour and attitudes so that they are no longer a threat to society and can live a lawful life back in society. This requires education to make punishment effective.
	There are common discussions about reparation or restoration as an aim for punishment. This is a combination of parts of retribution and reform. Restorative justice means the criminal must go through some kind of hardship or work to make up for what he or she has done. This may involve criminals repairing damage they caused or meeting victims of similar crimes to develop an understanding of how their actions harmed other people.

Christian responses

Reparation and retribution

Parts of the Bible suggest a degree of retribution or reparation. In Jesus' time this was thought to mean that some payment would be made equivalent to the injury or loss done. Some Christians use this to justify quite strict dealings with criminals.

Beliefs and teachings

'If anyone injures his neighbour, whatever he has done, must be done to him: fracture for fracture, eye for eye, tooth for tooth. As he has injured the other so he is to be injured ...'

Leviticus 24:19–20

Forgiveness and non-retaliation

Jesus' teaching on forgiveness and non-retaliation may seem incredible by today's standards.

Forgiving others was central to Jesus' life; he asked God to forgive as

Objectives

Identify different aims and different forms of punishment.

Explain Christian beliefs about forgiveness and non-retaliation with regard to punishment.

Key terms

Retribution: to 'get your own back' on the criminal, based on the Old Testament teaching of 'an eye for an eye'. An aim of punishment.

Deterrence: to put people off committing crimes. One of the aims of punishment.

Protection: to stop the criminal hurting anyone in society, an aim of punishment.

Reformation: to change someone's behaviour for the better. An aim of punishment.

Discussion activities

1 Why do you think we punish? Is it to get back at the person, in reparation for what was done, to deter others, to protect others, or to reform the criminal.

2 What might a Christian believe punishment should be about?

B *Reform is one of the aims of punishment*

You have heard that it was said, 'Eye for eye, and tooth for tooth.' But I tell you, Do not resist an evil person. If someone strikes you on the right cheek, turn to him the other also.

Matthew 5:38–39

Then Peter came to Jesus and asked, 'Lord, how many times shall I forgive my brother when he sins against me? Up to seven times? Jesus answered, 'I tell you, not seven times, but seventy-seven times.

Matthew 18:21–22

Do not judge, or you too will be judged. For in the same way as you judge others, you will be judged, and with the measure you use, it will be measured to you.

Matthew 7:1–2

Father forgive them, they do not know what they are doing.

Luke 23:34

he was dying on the cross, rather than seeking revenge. Retribution, like revenge, does not seem to be upheld by the Gospel message, even though it seems to be part of the Old Testament teaching.

Justice and righteous anger

This does not mean there is no call for any punishment. Justice is part of Christian values expressed in the Beatitudes (Matthew 23). Jesus expressed anger towards those who defiled sacred places (in the Temple in John 2:12–25) but he rejected punishment for its own sake, because we are all sinners (John 8:7). The Church emphasises the salvation of all souls, including those who have sinned or committed crimes.

◼ Crime prevention

A society which is fair and just is likely to suffer from less crime than one which is unfair and unjust. Christian values promote working towards a just society and the prevention of crime.

◯◯ links

For more about Christian teachings on forgiveness, see the Parable of the Forgiving Father on page 71.

> 66 *Punishment must have a constructive and redemptive purpose.* 99
>
> (Responsibility, Rehabilitation, and Restoration: A Catholic Perspective on Crime and Criminal Justice.)

◯◯ links

Christians should help those who suffer as a result of crime: see the Parable of the Good Samaritan on page 88.

AQA Examiner's tip

Make sure you are able to explain clearly the different aims of punishment and give examples.

Activities

1 Discuss which of these statements you most strongly agree with. Which do you most strongly disagree with? Give reasons.

   a 'Sometimes people do things so terrible that should be locked up for the rest of their lives.'

   b 'It is easier to think of those who have committed serious crimes as monsters, than face the reality that, given their life experiences, we may have gone exactly the same way.'

   c 'The good of the many outweighs the good of the few, so we should play safe and keep criminals in prison.'

   d 'If we decide that some people can never be forgiven, then there is no hope for any of us!'

   e 'Why bother trying to reform people who have done terrible things! They blew their chance. They should suffer!'

2 Decide which statements you think most closely reflect Christian teachings and justify your answers.

Summary

You should now understand that Christians believe punishment should involve forgiveness, justice, and reform.

Types of punishment

How do we punish people?

In the past punishments were physically brutal and severe. Theft of food could lead to long imprisonment. Many villages had stocks where transgressors might be chained to be ill-treated and ridiculed.

Today punishment usually restricts a person's freedom. Recently the UK has increased the number of crimes leading to a prison sentence and so prison numbers are rising. It is also the case that many people in prison suffer from mental health illnesses and many have very poor educational levels.

As well as **imprisonment** and **community service**, there are other forms of punishment including, for instance, fines for driving offences and more limited forms of restriction such as electronic tagging.

Objectives

Know and understand different types of punishment, their advantages and disadvantages.

Apply Christian beliefs about punishment to the types of punishment.

Key terms

Imprisonment: a method of punishment. Taking away a person's freedom, usually in prison.

Community service: a method of punishment. Forcing a person to undertake work for the community.

A   *Arguments about methods of punishment*

Method	For	Against
Imprisonment More serious crimes such as violent assault, rape and murder bring prison sentences. The restriction of a person's freedom is both a punishment and a deterrent and also protects the community while the person is in prison. It may also allow for reform if there are education facilities available.	■ Prison stops people from committing more crimes and so protects society. ■ Long prison sentences are a deterrent for more serious crimes.	■ Prisons are overcrowded; educational facilities are poor so prisoners are not reformed. ■ The majority of prisoners re-offend after they have been released. Prison does not protect society in the long run. ■ More people are sent to prison than ever before but crime levels are high. It is not much of a deterrent. ■ Prisons are academies of crime for new criminals to learn from more experienced criminals and develop drug dependencies.
Fines	■ Taking money from the offender is a deterrent. ■ The money raised can be used for society as a whole.	■ For the rich the fine has little deterrence. ■ For the poor the fine could be much harder and take money from dependents, such as children.
Community service Community service refers to compulsory work for the community such as cleaning, tending to public gardens or other forms of work for the public good. This is a more public act of 'paying back' for the crime committed. The public are able to see the criminal working for what they have done wrong.	■ It actually requires the criminal to do something for the community that he/she has harmed. ■ It provides them with an opportunity to do something productive which may help them begin to change their lives. ■ It is more effective for lesser crimes than imprisonment.	■ It is a soft option which does not cause much real discomfort to the criminal. ■ It is nothing to fear so does not act as a deterrent.

Discussion activity

1 Consider the following forms of punishment:

a prison
b community service
c fine
d forced to face their victim
e physical beating, restriction of movement (electronic tagging)
f public humiliation (being put in stocks).

Which aims do you think they each serve? Which do you think a Christian might be in favour of?

Activities

1 Consider the arguments for and against each type of punishment. Add to them if you can. Which do you think is the most convincing argument in each case? Give reasons for your decision.

2 Which aims of punishment do the methods considered here fulfil? Give detailed explanations of the links that you make.

AQA   Examiner's tip

Although you do not need to know the story of the assassination attempt on John Paul II it may help you to understand a Christian response to crime.

Prison chaplaincy

Prison chaplaincy can be described as a response to the Gospel call, 'I was in prison and you visited me.' Prisons have a Catholic chaplain to provide sacramental and pastoral care for residents and staff. The chaplains work for the spiritual, emotional and practical needs of all those in their care. They provide links with outside communities so that people leaving prison can find support and encouragement. Chaplains invite people to share in their ministry by training volunteers to become prison visitors. They work alongside both Christian and colleagues of other faiths.

Case study

Pope John Paul II forgave the man who tried to kill him

On 13 May 1982 Mehmet Ali Ağca shot and seriously wounded Pope John Paul II in the Vatican. He was convicted of the crime and served 20 years in prison. After the shooting, Pope John Paul II asked that people 'pray for my brother (Ağca), whom I have sincerely forgiven.' Later, in 1983, The Pope met and spoke with Ağca in prison. The Pope stayed in touch with Ağca's family, meeting his mother in 1987 and his brother ten years later. Ağca developed a friendship with the Pope and wrote a letter to him wishing him well in 2005, during the Pope's illness.

Case study

B   _Pope John Paul II with Mehmet Ali Ağca_

Activities

3 How did the Pope's actions reflect Christian teachings? (refer to pages 74–75)

4 Apply Christian teachings to the types of punishment described in Table **A**. What Christian aims might prison or community service serve?

Summary

You should now understand that different types of punishment have advantages and disadvantages.

Discussion activities 👤👤👤

1. What crimes should carry the death penalty: murder (or only the most terrible or multiple murders), violent rape, terrorism and drug trafficking, or none of these?
2. Is the death penalty worse than imprisoning someone for life?
3. Should a Christian oppose the death penalty in all situations?

Objectives

Know and understand arguments for and against the death penalty.

Investigate the Catholic Church's teaching on the death penalty.

■ The death penalty across the world

The **death penalty**, or **capital punishment**, is the execution of a criminal by the government. According to Amnesty International, in 2006 1,591 people were executed in 25 countries. Across the world:

- 88 countries, including the UK, have abolished the death penalty for all crimes
- 11 countries have abolished the death penalty for all but exceptional crimes
- 29 retain the death penalty in law but have not carried out any executions for more than 10 years
- 69 other countries retain and use the death penalty.

In a 2008 poll, 99% of almost 100,000 *Sun* readers voted in favour of a return to the death penalty. One reader's opinion was that since criminals take away the human rights of their victims when they commit a crime it is fair to take away the criminal's rights in return, in order to punish them.

Key terms

Death penalty/capital punishment: form of punishment in which a prisoner is put to death for crimes committed.

■ Arguments for and against the death penalty

A

Arguments for the death penalty	Arguments against the death penalty
■ It permanently removes the worst criminals, leaving society safer.	■ The death penalty contradicts the most basic human right to life. It is inhumane and makes the government a killer.
■ It is likely to be cheaper than imprisoning a person for life	■ The method of execution can be torturously painful.
■ It offers retribution, a life for a life.	■ Some countries with the death penalty have higher rates of murder than those without the death penalty – it doesn't seem to deter.
■ Fear of the death penalty may deter other potential killers. Singapore, which often carries out death sentences, has less serious crime.	■ Innocent people may be executed by mistake. If evidence is discovered after the execution has taken place, it will be too late.
■ If someone murders someone else, they have given up their human rights, including the one to stay alive themselves.	■ It may be that a person has killed someone. However, there may be special circumstances, like self defence.
■ It 'fits the crime' of murder – if you have killed, you should be killed as well.	■ The families and friends of those waiting for the death penalty suffer even thought they are innocent.
■ The most serious criminals only understand the language of violence.	■ The death penalty brutalises society, lowering respect for human life.
	■ Alternatives to the death penalty, such as life imprisonment may reform the criminal.

4 Consider these arguments from Christian perspectives and use them for a discussion.

a 'As Christians we have a duty to protect the weak in society and sometimes that means removing the most terrible criminals. The death penalty does this.'

b 'As a Christian I believe that all killing is wrong. God said so in the commandments.'

c 'The Old Testament says an eye for an eye a tooth for tooth.'

d 'Jesus taught that we should love our enemies and forgive the sins of others! The death penalty cannot do either of these.'

B Is life imprisonment more or less humane than execution?

■ Catholic teaching on the death penalty

The Catholic Church is largely opposed to the death penalty. On very rare occasions, the death penalty may be justified if it is the only way to protect society.

However, if alternative non-lethal methods are sufficient to defend and protect people's safety from the aggressor, then these are to be used instead as they better respect the dignity of the human person.

Many Christians are deeply opposed to the death penalty in any situation because they have a deep commitment to the sanctity of all human life and a belief in the morality of the commandment 'do not kill' and Jesus' command to love your neighbour.

Beliefs and teachings

the traditional teaching of the Church does not exclude recourse to the death penalty, if this is the only possible way of effectively defending human lives against the unjust aggressor.

Catechism 2267

❝ We cannot teach that killing is wrong by killing. ❞

US Catholic Bishops, 1994

❝ The death penalty is cruel and unnecessary. ❞

Pope John Paul II, 1999

Activities

1 What is capital punishment?

2 Suggest three strong arguments in favour of capital punishment and three strong arguments against capital punishment?

3 Consider these two statements and give reasons for each view. Which do you think is more convincing and why?

a 'The Catholic position on the death penalty means in practical terms that it is prohibited.'

b 'The Catholic position on the death penalty does not adequately uphold the dignity of the human person.'

AQA Examiner's tip

Be clear that while Catholic teaching does not rule capital punishment out completely, it is not approved of and in almost all cases thought to be unnecessary.

Summary

You should now understand that Christians have different views on the issue of the death penalty. The Catholic Church is opposed to the death penalty in almost all circumstances.

4.9 Prejudice and discrimination

Discussion activities

1. Should we give different educational opportunities to girls and boys (for instance allowing boys to play football and girls to play netball, allowing girls to do food technology while boys do engineering)?

2. Do people fear what they do not understand?

Objectives

Define prejudice and discrimination, give examples of each and explain how one is related to the other.

Suggest different kinds of prejudice and discrimination, and possible causes.

Know and understand relevant UK law.

Understand and be able to explain links between Biblical texts and Christian teaching on prejudice and discrimination.

■ Prejudice and discrimination

Prejudice is an attitude of mind. It means having a prejudgment or believing in a stereotype which is not based on fact. Common prejudices might include the belief that black men are good at dancing, women are not able to have leadership jobs in society, all Jewish men have beards, or all Japanese people are very efficient workers.

Discrimination means acting on prejudice and unfairly treating someone. Discrimination might include paying a woman less than a man for the same job, not giving a person a job because of their skin colour, not allowing an employee to use the till in a shop because they are a different race from you. Discrimination is an action which is based on prejudice; it is often against the law.

Key terms

Prejudice: unfairly judging someone before the facts are known. Holding biased opinions about an individual of group.

Discrimination: to act against someone on the basis of sex, race, religion, etc. Discrimination is usually seen as wrong.

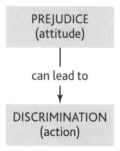

PREJUDICE
(attitude)

|
can lead to
↓

DISCRIMINATION
(action)

 A   *Prejudice and discrimination*

Prejudice and discrimination can be based on many different aspects of a person's identity such as age (against youth or the elderly), religion and belief, disability, gender, race and sexual orientation (whether a person is homosexual or heterosexual).

Prejudice and discrimination reflect:

- inequality: not seeing another person as equal to you
- fear: being nervous or uncomfortable with difference
- ignorance: a lack of knowledge and understanding about those who are different.

In societies which are made up of people of many different cultures, races and religions, prejudice and discrimination can cause problems.

B   *An example of prejudice is assuming that a girl is not good at football*

Discussion activity

3. Is discrimination worse than prejudice?

Christian perspectives on and prejudice and discrimination

Christian beliefs about and attitudes towards prejudice and discrimination come chiefly from the Bible.

The Catholic Church teaches that all human beings are created with the image and likeness of God (Genesis 1) and are creatures of God (Psalms 139:14–18) so should have human rights and equality.

Beliefs and teachings

Every form of social or cultural discrimination in fundamental personal rights on the grounds of sex, race, colour, social conditions, language, or religion must be curbed and eradicated as incompatible with God's design.

Catechism 1935

Access to employment and to professions must be open to all without unjust discrimination: men and women, healthy and disabled, natives and immigrants.

Catechism 2433

Legislation on prejudice and discrimination in the UK

The Equality and Human Rights Commission is the UK's government body responsible for working towards the elimination of discrimination, the reduction of inequality and the protection of human rights, so that everyone has a fair chance to participate in society.

Equality and discrimination rights

C

Age	It is unlawful for your age to be the cause of less favourable treatment in your workplace or in vocational training.
Religion and belief	Your religion or belief, or those of somebody else, should not interfere with your right to be treated fairly at work, at school, in shops or while accessing public services such as health care and housing.
Disability	If you have a physical or mental impairment, you have specific rights that protect you against discrimination. Employers and service providers are obliged to make adjustments for you.
Gender	Women, men and transgender people should not be treated unfairly because of their gender, because they are married or because they are raising a family.
Race	Wherever you were born, wherever your parents came from, whatever the colour of your skin, you have a right to be treated fairly and equally.
Sexual orientation	Whether you are gay, lesbian, bisexual or heterosexual should not put you at a disadvantage.

From the Equality and Human rights commission, www.equalityhumanrights.com

Beliefs and teachings

Love your neighbour as yourself.

Matthew 22:39

There is neither Jew nor Greek, slave nor free, male nor female, for you are all one in Christ Jesus.

Galatians 3:28

Activities

1. How do Biblical texts inform Catholic teaching on prejudice and discrimination?
2. How should this teaching affect the attitudes of Christians?
3. What sorts of things might Christians do as a result of this teaching?

AQA Examiner's tip

Although you do not need to know the information in Table C for the exam, this shows how alert current UK law is to religious teaching.

Summary

You should now know that prejudice is an attitude of mind which prejudges a person and which may lead to actions which treat people unfairly (discrimination). The Bible promotes love and equality and the Catholic Church teaches that all human beings have human rights and dignity and so prejudice and discrimination are wrong.

4.10 Race and colour

Racism in the UK

Racism is prejudice and discrimination based on a person's race or skin colour. Racism is a serious problem in British society and beyond. A 2002 Government report concluded racist attitudes are 'prevalent' across the country, though they are concentrated more in the north and among older, poorer and less educated white people.

Racism has lead to riots in British cities, as well as increasing hate crimes of a racial character (crimes based on or influenced by racist attitudes).

Case study

Stephen Lawrence

Stephen Lawrence was a black British teenager from South-East London. He was stabbed to death while waiting for a bus on the evening of 22nd April 1993. After an investigation, five suspects were arrested but never convicted. In 1999, Sir William MacPherson conducted an inquiry into the Metropolitan police investigation and concluded that the force was 'institutionally racist', that is that there were deep-rooted prejudices which led to discrimination in the way that racially-motivated crimes were investigated.

A *Stephen Lawrence*

Case study

Teenager faces 13 years for racist killing of Asian

In April 2000, Shiblu Rahman, was found by his wife in the doorway of his home, on his hands and knees, having been stabbed and beaten. The attack occurred during the early hours of the morning as Mr Rahman returned home from work. The judge said that he 'was hard working and everybody liked him. His wife and two children, aged four years and five months, were at home.' A loving husband and father, Mr Rahman was said to have exclaimed during the attack: 'Why me? What have I done to you?' The police said: 'it was a purely racist motive.' The teenager who stabbed Mr Rahman was sentenced to life imprisonment for a racially aggravated murder. Along with three other youths, he had harassed Mr Rahman before this attack, calling him a 'Paki'.

B *UK race law*

The Race Relations Act (1965)	Made it unlawful to refuse access to anyone on racial grounds to public places such as hotels, restaurants, pubs, cinemas or public transport
	Made stirring up racial hatred (incitement) a criminal offence
The Race Relations Act (1976)	Made discrimination an offence and gave those affected by it compensation through employment tribunals and the courts
Amendment to the Race Relations Act (2001)	Made it compulsory for public bodies, including local authorities, to have policies based on the equal treatment of all

Christian responses to racism

The Catholic Church teaches that racism is evil and destructive because:

- it denies the belief that all humans reflect the image of God and have dignity (Genesis 1)
- it contradicts the teaching of love of neighbour (Matthew 22:39)
- it contradicts the belief that all are one in Christ (Galatians 3:28).

Christians are called to live their lives according to these teachings. The Church teaches that Christians should not support racist organisations in any way. Some Christians are involved in anti-racist organisations such as the Catholic Association for Racial Justice.

⚭ links

For the full text of Galatians 3:28, see page 81.

Case study

Catholic Association for Racial Justice

'We are a movement of Catholics from diverse backgrounds that are committed to working together for racial justice both within our Church and within our society. This unites and defines us and establishes the context within which we speak.'

Catholic Association for Racial Justice

CARJ works to empower black and ethnic minority Catholics. It works with Catholic Dioceses, parishes and schools, raising awareness of issues of racism and racial justice, promoting discussion, reflection and action, and promoting the annual Racial Justice Sunday within the Church. It develops links with people from other Churches and other faiths. It responds to requests for advice and support from those who are the victims of racial injustice and discrimination.

C *CARJ respresentatives visit schools to raise awareness of racism.*

Activities

1. What does the Catholic Church teach about racism?
2. In what ways does UK law support Christian teachings on racism?
3. How might a Christian respond to the Church's teachings on racism in their daily lives?

AQA Examiner's tip

Remember that you do not need to learn the UK law on racism or the examples of racism included here, but you do need be able to see how Christians might respond to these issues.

Summary

You should now know that UK law makes many acts of racial discrimination illegal. The Catholic Church teaches that racism is evil, contrary to God's law.

Gender and disability

Prejudice and discrimination about gender

Prejudice and discrimination on the basis of **gender** means not treating men and women equally and not giving men and women equal opportunities. Historically many cultures and civilisations gave men positions of power and control in public life, and gave them more rights and legal protections than women. Today, some people continue to express sexist attitudes and treat people unfairly (discriminate) because of their gender. For example:

- Women are paid less than men on average and in some cases they are paid less than men get in the same jobs.
- While women make up more than 50 per cent of the workforce men hold a greater proportion of senior positions.
- Often when people hear the word 'doctor' they think of a man. When they hear the word 'nurse' they think of a woman. This may reflect an expectation that the man will hold the senior medical position.

Gender discrimination in religion

Religion sometimes reflects these attitudes towards women:

- Until relatively recently women were not allowed to serve on the altar in the Catholic Church, and not allowed to be Readers or Eucharistic ministers.
- In some parts of the world, women attending church must cover their heads.
- Some Christians believe that men are the head of the family and that women should mainly stay at home and look after the children.

Catholic teaching against prejudice and discrimination about gender

Catholic teaching rejects any suggestion that women are not equal.

The Church teaches that there are differences between men and women and that they have distinctive roles in the religious life of the Church (for instance only men can be priests). However women must not be discriminated against unfairly. Women, as well as men, were made in the image of God.

Activities

1 Find out the proportion of the staff in your school or college who are male and female. Then look at the senior positions in your school. (heads, deputies, assistant heads). Is the male to female proportion the same among ordinary teachers and senior teachers? If not, why not? Do you think this is a matter of prejudice or discrimination? Might there be other reasons for the proportions?

2 Why might some people say that the Catholic Church does not practise what it preaches when it comes to gender discrimination? How might the Church respond to this accusation?

Objectives

Suggest ways in which people are discriminated against on the basis of gender and disability.

Explain UK law and Catholic teaching on gender and disability discrimination.

Suggest ways in which Christians might respond to issues of gender and disability discrimination.

Key terms

Gender: another word for a person's sex (male, female).

Discussion activities

1 Why do you think women used to be paid less than men for the same work?

2 Some argue that society and the media has a problem with disability. What sort of problem do you think this might be?

Beliefs and teachings

God gives man and woman an equal personal dignity. Man is a person, man and woman equally so, since both were created in the image and likeness of the personal God.

Catechism 2334

■ Prejudice and discrimination about disability

A disabled person is someone with 'a physical or mental impairment which has a substantial and long-term adverse effect on his ability to carry out normal day-to-day activities' (The Disability Discrimination Act 2005). These impairments include: cancer, diabetes, multiple sclerosis, hearing or sight impairments, a mobility difficulty, mental health conditions or learning difficulties. UK law promotes **disability** equality. However there are many ways in which society today presents fully able people as normal and disability as a lower kind of humanity, for example:

- The media presents images of human perfection in magazines and on TV – photographs are digitally manipulated to remove supposed imperfections. It often seems as if a disabled person cannot be a beautiful person.
- Physically disabled people sometimes do not have the same opportunities in work or education.
- People with mental illness face widespread discrimination from employers, even though 1 in 6 people suffer from mental illness at some point in their life.
- There are increasing concerns that unborn babies detected as having disabilities may be aborted.

Christian responses to prejudice and discrimination about disability

Catholic teaching on disability is based on the belief that all are one in Christ, that all are made in the image and likeness of God, and that all should be loved. Traditional responses to people with disabilities tended to see them as weak recipients of charity. However, people with disabilities are still in the image of God and should not just be seen as passive receivers of charity, but active members of the Church.

The Church is seeking to remove all barriers to full participation in the life of the Church – for example, Bibles in Braille, celebrations with provision for the deaf. Children with disabilities must have their rights protected in education and families with disabled children should be supported materially and spiritually.

A　*Does your local Catholic Church ever offer a signed Mass for the deaf?*

Key terms

Disability: when a person has a mental or physical condition that limits movement or activities.

Activities

3　How are people discriminated against on the basis of gender and disability?

4　What does the Catholic Church teach about gender and disability discrimination?

5　How might a Catholic parish church ensure that it includes both women and people with disabilities in its activities? Make some suggestions about how participation and access can be improved.

AQA　Examiner's tip

Make sure that you can give specific examples of prejudice and discrimination as well as general explanations.

Summary

You should now know that the Catholic Church is opposed to discrimination on grounds of gender and disability on the basis of beliefs about the dignity and equality of every human being.

Prejudice and discrimination over religion

In the UK

Some people experience prejudice and discrimination because they belong to a religious group. A Government report in 2002 concluded that Muslim men of Pakistani and Bangladeshi background are more likely to be unemployed compared to other Asians. Pakistani Muslims are three times more likely to be jobless than Hindus are. Indian Muslims are twice as likely to be unemployed as Indian Hindus. There are reports of attacks on Jewish graveyards and many religious discrimination cases in the courts.

In the world

Throughout the world there are examples of very serious religious discrimination. Some countries have an official state religion and members of other religions are not allowed to express their religious beliefs, or build places of worship. Some countries prohibit religious items such as Bibles, crosses and rosaries.

Case study

Freedom of religion in China

The Chinese government recognises the right to believe, but limits worship to a government-controlled system of controlled churches, congregations, mosques, monasteries, and temples. The official registration process requires government checking and Christians who have refused to follow the official procedures and have attended Bible Study meetings have been arrested. Leaders of such underground churches are sometimes held on fabricated charges.

(Human Rights Watch World Report, 2008, p.267, http://hrw.org/wr2k8/pdfs/wr2k8_web.pdf)

The right to religious freedom and freedom from discrimination on grounds of religion

Under UK human rights laws, a religious believer should be able to hold and practise their faith freely, and a person should have the right to have no faith. This means they can believe in their own religion and they can live out their religious life in public, as long as it does not restrict the rights and freedoms of others. In 2006 the Equality Act of 2006 made it unlawful for someone to discriminate against you because of your religion or belief (or because you have no religion or belief).

Activities

Examples of religious discrimination cases in the UK

1 Consider the cases on page 87. For each one, explain the kind of religious discrimination which is taking place.

2 What is the alternative argument in each of these cases?

Objectives

Identify examples of religious discrimination in the UK and throughout the world.

Consider arguments for and against the public expression of religion.

Know and understand Catholic teaching on religious freedom and discrimination.

Discussion activities

1 Should religion be kept out of public life (such as schools and the workplace)?

2 If you have a religious belief which means you feel you should wear a particular piece of clothing or item (such as Hijab for Muslims, a Turban for Sikh men, a cross for a Christian) should you be allowed to wear it in public, at work and in school?

Research activity

Human Rights Watch

Visit Human Rights Watch online (http://hrw.org) and download the latest *World Report*. When the report comes up, do a search for the word 'religious' in the various country reports. Find three examples of what you would consider serious religious discrimination and make notes on the details.

a Girl wins religious bangle row

In July 2008, Sarika Singh won her battle with a school in South Wales, over her right to wear a religious bangle at school. The school excluded and segregated the 14 year old on the grounds that she was breaking the school's 'no jewellery policy'. The high court agreed with Sarika that she had been a victim of unlawful discrimination and that the bangle was an expression of her Sikh faith.

b Ladele v London Borough of Islington

Lillian Ladele worked for Islington council as a registrar, and part of her duties included registering marriages. With the introduction of civil partnerships in the UK, Ladele's responsibilities also came to include the registering of civil (same sex) partnerships. Ladele, a practising Christian, asked to be excused from performing a role in such ceremonies. Ladele felt that it would be wrong to act as a witness to these civil partnerships when they were not in line with her Christian faith.

Two gay members of staff felt victimised by her decision. They felt that Ladele's actions demonstrated discrimination against the gay community, and made a formal complaint. The council concluded that Ladele was in breach of their 'dignity for all' policy, and subsequently took disciplinary action against her. Ladele claimed that the way she was treated by the council should be considered bullying and harassment.

In an employment tribunal, the tribunal upheld Ladele's complaint that she had been discriminated against because of her religion. The tribunal ruled that her employer had 'placed greater value on the rights of the lesbian, gay, bisexual and transsexual community than it placed on the rights of Ms Ladele'.

A *Arguments for and against the public expression of religious beliefs*

Arguments for	Arguments against
Religion is not just about what is going on in your head. It is also about how those beliefs affect how you live your life. If you do not allow people to express their religious beliefs, then you are oppressing them.	In a plural society, there will be greater tension if people are allowed to express their religious beliefs in public. Religion is better kept private.
If you restrict the public expression of faith, you are saying that that faith or faith in general is bad.	If people are allowed to wear religious dress in the workplace and in schools, some religious people might feel they must be more outward about their religion, even if they would rather not.
Human rights guarantee religious freedoms. This is because in the past people were persecuted terribly on account of their religion. These rights must be defended.	It is more important we emphasise in public what is common between us rather than emphasis our differences.

■ Catholic teaching on religious freedom and discrimination

At the Second Vatican Council, the Catholic Church made the 'Declaration of Religious Freedom', in which it taught that human rights are based on the dignity of the human person. A human being should be free to believe and not be forced to act in a way that is contrary to their beliefs, either in private or in public.

In the New Testament St Paul was sometimes persecuted because of his Christian faith, and many of the first Christians were persecuted because of their religion. Jesus showed acts of kindness to people of another religion, such as the Samaritan women at the well.

Summary

You should now know that the Catholic Church supports the human rights to religious freedom and teaches that a person should not be forced to do things that go against his or her religious beliefs.

4.13 The Parable of the Good Samaritan

Discussion activities

A French journalist conducted an experiment in the Paris Metro. Actors, pretending to be a mugger and a victim, acted out muggings throughout the day at one of the busiest stations. For the most part, people walked by doing nothing at all, even through the attacks were in plain view. The vast majority of people did nothing. They did not call the police and they did not intervene.

1 Why do you think so many people did nothing at all?

2 Do you think you would have done something?

3 What was the point of this experiment, do you think?

Objectives

Describe the main features of the parable and suggest how Christians might interpret it.

Suggest how Christians might act in response to the parable.

Key terms

Samaritans: the Samaritans were mixed race Jews. They regarded each other as enemies, so in Luke's Parable of the Good Samaritan, the Samaritan had no obligation to help the injured Jew.

Christian attitudes to the disadvantaged in society

The example above shows how easy it is to ignore the plight of others. Christian values identify the importance of addressing the needs of the poor and disadvantaged in society by standing up to injustice. The Parable of the Good Samaritan is a story about what it means to be a follower of Christ.

Background

The Parable is set on the road from Jerusalem down to Jericho. There was great hatred between Jews and Samaritans. Samaritans had over the course of history intermarried with non-Jews and developed their own religious practices, so they were viewed as having left the faith. Priests who were not on duty in the temple had homes in Jericho. Priests also had to take care not to come into contact with blood as this would have made them impure for a time and unable to perform priestly duties.

A Map showing Samaria – the area where the Samaritans lived

The Parable of the Good Samaritan

Beliefs and teachings

On one occasion an expert in the law stood up to test Jesus. 'Teacher, he asked, what must I do to inherit eternal life?' 'What is written in the Law?' he replied. 'How do you read it?' He answered: 'Love the Lord your God with all your heart and with all your soul and with all your strength and with all your mind'; and, 'Love your neighbour as yourself. 'You have answered correctly,' Jesus replied. 'Do this and you will live'. But he wanted to justify himself, so he asked Jesus, 'And who is my neighbour?'

In reply Jesus said: 'A man was going down from Jerusalem to Jericho, when he fell into the hands of robbers. They stripped him of his clothes, beat him and went away, leaving him half-dead. A priest happened to be going down the same road, and when he saw the man,

he passed by on the other side. So too, a Levite, when he came to the place and saw him, passed by on the other side. But a Samaritan, as he travelled, came where the man was; and when he saw him, he took pity on him. He went to him and bandaged his wounds, pouring on oil and wine. Then he put the man on his own donkey, brought him to an inn and took care of him. The next day he took out two silver coins and gave them to the innkeeper. 'Look after him,' he said, 'and when I return, I will reimburse you for any extra expense you may have.'

Which of these three do you think was a neighbour to the man who fell into the hands of robbers?' The expert in the law replied, 'The one who had mercy on him'. Jesus told him, 'Go and do likewise.'

Luke 10:25–37

Activities

1. Who might the different people in the parable represent? Suggest two different possibilities for each person and give reasons for your suggestion.

2. In what ways might someone 'cross over to the other side of the road' today?

3. 'I never see anyone who has been mugged in the street. This parable hasn't got anything to say to me!' How do you think has this Christian failed to understand what the parable might be saying to him?

∞links

Consider how this parable might influence Christian responses to prejudice and discrimination on account of race, gender, disability and religion.

AQA   Examiner's tip

Make sure you know the parable and can apply it to different situations.

Interpreting the parable

There are many ways in which this parable may be interpreted and applied to Christian living. These include:

- Loving God and loving neighbour is at the centre of what it means to be a Christian and inherit eternal life. Thoughtlessly following ritual laws is not enough.
- Being a Christian demands action, not just beliefs.
- Christians have a duty to offer help to the disadvantaged – those who are rejected and ignored by society. The parable answers the question 'Who is my neighbour' by suggesting that anyone in need is a 'neighbour'.
- Listeners would have expected the Samaritan to be shown in bad light and the Priest and Levite in a good light. Jesus deliberately reverses this.
- Jesus stood with the poor and disadvantaged. He reached out to and picked up the wounded, cared for them and offered them healing.

As a result of reading this parable a Christian might:

- become involved in organisations dedicated to supporting members of society who are disadvantaged or discriminated against
- look at how their local parish might be inclusive to disadvantaged Christians. For instance by installing a wheelchair ramp, or having a signed Mass
- by making sure that Christians from all backgrounds are welcomed to church and able to participate in parish life.

B   The Good Samaritan?

Activities

4. In what ways are the interpretations of the parable different?

5. How might a Christian apply the parable to the way in which they may see others?

6. Read the parable again. What meanings do you think it has for you today?

Summary

You should now understand that the Parable of the Good Samaritan challenges Christians to consider how they look upon others in society, especially those who are different from themselves. It calls Christians to consider in what ways they should respond to those in need, particularly the disadvantaged in society.

4

The Sacrament of reconciliation – summary

For the examination you should now be able to:

✔ explain the terms sin, reconciliation, punishment, prejudice and discrimination

✔ explain the Christian beliefs about sin and forgiveness

✔ understand why and how Catholics celebrate the Sacrament of Reconciliation and explain its symbolism

✔ explain how the parable of the Forgiving Father relates to the Sacrament of Reconciliation

✔ explain the causes and effects of crime

✔ outline Christian beliefs about crime and punishment

✔ explain the different aims of punishments and some forms of punishment

✔ explain different Christian attitudes towards the death penalty

✔ outline Christians beliefs about prejudice and discrimination, and different Christian responses to racism, religious, gender and disability discrimination and prejudice.

Sample answer

1 Write an answer to the following exam question.

Outline the Rite of the Sacrament of Reconciliation in the Roman Catholic Church. *(6 marks)*

2 Read the following sample answer:

> Catholics believe that when they have sinned they need to be forgiven by God so they go to confession. At confession they say sorry for their sins and they ask God to forgive them. They promise they won't do it again and the Priest forgives them saying a prayer. Afterwards they may say some prayers too.

3 With a partner, discuss the sample answer. Do you think that there are other things that the student could have included in the answer?

4 What mark would you give this answer out of 6? Look at the marks scheme in the Introduction on page 7 (AO1). What are the reasons for the mark you have given?

AQA Examination-style questions

1 Look at the illustration and answer the following questions.

(a) What is meant by the word reconciliation?

(2 marks)

(b) Explain what the Roman Catholic Church teaches about the causes of crime.

(4 marks)

(c) Explain the effects of crime on individuals and society.

(6 marks)

(d) 'The death penalty is sometimes necessary'
Do you agree? Give reasons for your answer, showing that you have thought about more than one point of view. Refer to Roman Catholic teaching in your answer.

(6 marks)

AQA Examiner's tip Remember, when asked to give an example of Roman Catholic teaching, you should try to refer to the Bible and to Church teachings, linking the two together if you are able.

5 Christian healing

5.1 Christian attitudes to sickness and healing

Discussion activities 👥

1. In what ways can people suffer?
2. Why can sickness be challenging for a Christian to accept?
3. Why do you think many Christians see Jesus as a healer?
4. How should we act for the sick and dying in society today?

■ God in human suffering

Suffering is a real challenge to human life. People ask, why is there sickness? Why do people suffer? Suffering can cause real anger and even despair, and so for many Christians it is difficult to understand. In the Bible, Jeremiah asks what must be a common question, 'Why is my pain unending and my wound grievous and incurable?' (Jeremiah 15:18).

> 66 The sick and the handicapped have a place in God's plan. We do not see or understand that plan. We are often baffled by the suffering that so many sick and handicapped must endure, and especially so when it occurs in our own family. We have to trust in God's great love and in his goodness, and never give up doing so. 99
>
> Cardinal Basil Hume, 1984

Activity

1. Compare these two Christian attitudes towards suffering and sickness in life.
   a. 'The reason you are sick is because you have too little faith! If you really believe you will get better!'
   b. 'Suffering is part of the mystery of life. You can't make sense of why it happens, you should just put your faith in God that he will give the strength to see it through.'

   What are the merits of each view? Which is more helpful in your opinion, and why?

■ Jesus and healing

God is traditionally seen as a healer, and the healing of the sick is central to Jesus' ministry. Wherever Jesus went, people brought the sick to him to be healed. Jesus said, 'It is not the healthy who need a doctor, but the sick. I have not come to call the righteous, but sinners.' (Mark 2:17).

Objectives

Know and understand different Christian attitudes to sickness and healing.

Explain the importance of healing to Jesus' ministry and how the Church interprets Jesus' command to heal the sick.

Identify the three Sacraments of the Sick.

A *Human suffering is a mystery*

Beliefs and teachings

A man with leprosy came to him and begged him on his knees, If you are willing, you can make me clean. Filled with compassion, Jesus reached out his hand and touched the man. 'I am willing,' he said. 'Be clean!' Immediately the leprosy left him and he was cured.

Mark 1:40–42

Healing in St Mark's Gospel

Other examples of Jesus' healing from St Mark's Gospel include:

- 1:21–28 Jesus drives out an unclean spirit
- 1:29–31 The healing of Peter's mother-in-law
- 1:40–45 The healing of a leper
- 2:1–12 The healing of a paralysed man

The Church teaches that:

- Christ is the healer of our soul and body
- the compassion of Jesus for the sick and his many healings all point to the coming Kingdom of God and the victory over sin, suffering and death.

■ A command to heal the sick

Christians have a duty to care for those who are sick or weakened by old age. Visiting and caring for the sick, therefore, is an important part of Christian discipleship. When Christians show concern for the sick, they are:

- following the example of Jesus
- serving Jesus by looking after the poor and sick that they meet.

How does the Church show concern for the sick?

There are different ways in which the Church can show concern for the sick, such as:

- by visiting the sick
- by bringing people comfort through the sacrament of the Eucharist
- by praying and asking God to take care of them, especially in the hour of their death.

All baptised Christians should share in the ministry to the sick by:

- doing all they can to help the sick return to health
- showing love to the sick
- celebrating the sacraments with them.

■ The three Sacraments of the Sick

The Catholic Church describes three Sacraments of the Sick:

1. The communion of the sick (taking communion to those who are unable to attend Mass due to illness, disability or old age).
2. The Anointing of the Sick (where the priests visits the sick at home or in hospital).
3. Viaticum (A special Eucharist for a person close to death).

> 66 *Do not neglect the sick and elderly. Do not turn away from the handicapped and dying. Do not push them to the margins of society. For if you do, you fail to understand an important truth.* 99
>
> Pope John Paul II, at Southward, 1982

Activities

2. Why do Christians see serving the sick as serving Jesus?

3. Many of the images in the media today are of fit and healthy people. Health and fitness seem to be regarded as normal and yet many people will suffer illness in their lives and most will grow old and suffer some weakness in old age. Why do you think suffering is not seen as a normal part of life?

AQA Examiner's tip

Remember that there are three Sacraments of the Sick for different circumstances.

∞ links

For more about the Anointing of the Sick, see pages 94–95.

For more about Viaticum, see page 98.

Activities

4. How may Christians show concern for the sick?

5. What are the Sacraments of the Sick?

Summary

You should now understand that Christians see sickness and suffering in different ways. Healing was central to Jesus' ministry and the Church teaches that he commands Christians to care for the sick.

5.2 | Anointing of the Sick (extreme unction)

■ What is the Sacrament of the Anointing of the Sick?

The New Testament background

Jesus' apostles were sent out to anoint the sick. 'They drove out many demons and anointed many sick people with oil and healed them' (Mark 6:13).

An example of the Sacrament is found in the Letter of St James: 'Is any one of you sick? He should call the elders of the church to pray over him and anoint him with oil in the name of the Lord. And the prayer offered in faith will make the sick person well; the Lord will raise him up. If he has sinned, he will be forgiven' (James 5:14–15).

Four things are important here:

1 The religious leaders of the community are called to give the gift of healing.
2 The community prays for the sick person.
3 The sick person is **anointed** with oil.
4 The sacrament is done in the name of the Lord.

The Purpose of the Sacrament

Human life includes suffering and death. These present real challenges to living in faith – do suffering and death mark the end of life or a journey to something beyond this life? The Sacrament of **Anointing of the Sick** recognises the great mystery of suffering and death and offers a way of facing that great challenge.

Who is the Sacrament for?

The Sacrament is intended to bring healing and reconciliation to the seriously ill and the elderly or weak, not just those who are close to death. Here are some occasions when it might be administered:

- For those who are seriously ill.
- Before a person has surgery.
- To elderly people who are weakened by age even if they are not sick.
- For sick people who have lost consciousness.

Objectives

Know and understand the rite of the Anointing of the Sick.

Identify the main stages of the Sacrament, its symbolism and meaning.

Suggest the different possible effects of the Sacrament.

Key terms

Anointing: Being blessed with holy oil. This occurs during certain sacraments, e.g. the Anointing of the Sick.

Anointing of the Sick (extreme unction): a sacrament traditionally given to people who are dying, now also given to people who are ill or having an operation.

Laying on of hands: an ancient sign from the Bible symbolising the Holy Spirit giving the person gifts.

A *Anointing with oil is an ancient Christian practice*

Activities

1 Which stages of the Sacrament can be found in the account of James in James 5:14–15?

2 Look at Table **B** and devise a diagram which illustrates the stages of the Rite. Use different colours to show the meanings.

The rite

B

Stage	Description	Symbol and meaning
Sprinkling of holy water	The Priest sprinkles the people with holy water with the words: 'Let this water call to mind our baptism in Christ, who by his death and resurrection has redeemed us.'	A reminder of a person's baptism and that they are called to follow Christ.
The liturgy of the word	A short Gospel reading such as Matthew 11:25–30, Mark 2:1–12 or Luke 7:18–23.	Readings that show the healing power of Jesus, to remind the sick person of his power.
Laying on of hands	The priest lays his hands on the sick person, after recalling the words from the letter of James.	This symbolises: ■ the giving of strength ■ the gift of the Holy Spirit, who brings power to face suffering and death ■ the touch of healing.
Anointing with oil	The priest anoints the sick person's forehead and their hands with oil (usually in the shape of a cross), 'Through this holy anointing, may the Lord in his love and mercy help you with the grace of the Holy Spirit.' 'May the Lord who frees you from sin save you and raise you up.'	This is the third ceremony in which a person is anointed, the first being after baptism and the second after confirmation. This follows the instructions of St James. The oil symbolises God's blessing, his healing and comfort.
Liturgy of the Eucharist (optional)	The Eucharist may be offered, usually in the form of the body (bread) if the person is at home.	The Eucharist also brings the person into close contact with Christ and offers strength and healing.

The rite may be offered as part of a service at Church which the whole community can attend.

C Laying hands on the sick

D Anointing with oil

What are the effects of the Sacrament?

The emphasis of the Sacrament of the Sick is on restoration and healing. The Sacrament:

■ brings the power and love of the Holy Spirit

■ offers spiritual strength, comfort, peace and courage

■ offers the forgiveness of sins

■ may bring about the restoration of physical health

■ leads to spiritual healing

■ helps the person overcome the fear of death.

Summary

You should now understand the Rite of the Anointing of the Sick is an important rite in the Roman Catholic Church.

Beliefs and teachings

Father in heaven, through this holy anointing grant XXX comfort in his/her suffering. When he/she is afraid, give him/her courage, when afflicted, give him/her patience, when dejected, afford him/her hope, and when alone, assure him/her of the support of your holy people, through Christ our lord. Amen.

Prayer after anointing

AQA Examiner's tip

Make sure you are able to explain the different effects of the Sacrament, not just the hope of a miraculous cure.

Activities

3 Why might Christians find the Sacrament helpful?

4 Why might it be important for the parish to gather together to celebrate the Sacrament of the Anointing of the sick?

5.3 Attitudes to death and life after death

Discussion activities

1. What questions do people often ask about death?
2. Is it good or bad to think much about life after death?

Objectives

Explain Catholic teaching on death and the afterlife.

Suggest different Christian responses to death and life after death.

Death

Death is frequently described as the one certainty in life. Human life is finite; it will end. Death seems to be a terrible challenge to life. It is the constant, painful reminder that however beautiful our relationships are, as human relationships, they will come to an end. Death throws up fundamental questions: why must I die? Why do I fear death? In life, it may appear easier to try not to think about death.

A

> 66 *One day I shall die. Thinking about that is good for me. It helps me to look at the way I am living. It enables me to get a better perspective. I know that I shall not remain forever in this world.* 99
>
> Cardinal Basil Hume

Key terms

Resurrection: when Jesus rose from the dead after dying on the cross. That other people may experience resurrection is one of the key beliefs of Christianity.

Judgement: God deciding who should be saved on the basis of actions in this life.

Purgatory: the purification of sin from a person who has died so they can come close to God in Heaven.

Heaven: being with God after death.

Hell: being apart from God after death.

Activity

1. In what ways might this life be a preparation for the next life?

Christian beliefs about death

It is natural to fear death. Death symbolises the loss of everyone we love and loss of everything we know. Some people believe death means the end of everything. Others think that after death you are reborn again – this is reincarnation, a belief of Hinduism, Buddhism and Sikhism.

In Christianity there is a belief in **resurrection** and life after death. Catholic teachings state that death is not the end. There is an afterlife.

B *Is death the end or a beginning?*

C

The consequence of sin	The Bible suggests that death is a result of human sin. The book of Genesis in the Old Testament suggests that death came as a punishment for sin. In the New Testament, St Paul writes, 'Therefore, just as sin entered the world through one man, and death through sin, and in this way death came to all men, because all sinned' (Romans 5:12).
Transformed by Christ	The Catholic Church teaches that through his death, Jesus has conquered death, and so opened the possibility of salvation to all men. In his death, Jesus went down to hell and then returned. Jesus has *'opened up the gates of heaven'*. In other words, he has brought to people the possibility of life with God. Death is the end of the earthly pilgrimage towards God, but not the end. In death, God calls human beings to be with him.
Resurrection and new life	From the beginning of Christianity, belief in the resurrection has been essential. The Christian Church began after the women at the tomb and the apostles accepted that Jesus had risen from the dead. Jesus said 'I am the resurrection and the life. He who believes in me will live, even though he dies' (John 11:25).The Church teaches that after death the Christian gains a new body, not made of flesh.
Judgement	The Church teaches that all are **judged** after their death on the way they have lived their life and the ways they have served or not served God in loving their neighbour. It has been described by one priest as 'whispering into the ear of a merciful and compassionate God the story of my life which I have never been able to tell'.
Purgatory, the journey to God	The Catholic Church teaches that after death the person journeys towards the holiness of God. To do this most people must be purified of any remaining evil within them. **Purgatory** is this purification of sin. Prayers are said during the funeral mass to ask that the person will shortly be with God.
With God in Heaven	The Church teaches that **Heaven** is not a place, but it is to be in the presence of God. To be in Heaven is to be with Christ (see Phillippians 1:23; John 14:3; 1 Thessalonians 4:17). It is also where the saints and martyrs are, as well as all those who have passed through Purgatory. Heaven is a joyful eternal experience which cannot be described or imagined fully.
Hell	The Catholic Church says little about **Hell**. It does hold that Hell exists and is eternal. Hell is, for a Christian, a state of being without God. Those who die in a state of mortal sin 'descend into hell, where they suffer the punishments of hell' (Catechism 1035) which is mainly separation from God. The Church says nothing about who is in Hell, or indeed whether anyone is.

> 66 *We can walk away deliberately. We can choose self, self alone, above and before all. We shall live on, lonely, barren, empty, miserable lives. That is hell.* 99
>
> Cardinal Basil Hume

Activities

2   Using the information in Table **C**, explain in words you could use to a younger person what Christians believe about the afterlife.

3   What images are conjured up when you think of the word Hell? How similar or different are they from the suggestions given here? Are there any problems for a Christian about belief in Hell?

4   'For a Christian, death may be both feared and desired.' How can this view be true? Explain with reference to Christian beliefs about death and the afterlife.

AQA   Examiner's tip

The Catholic Church teaches some very clear things about death and the afterlife which are different from other religions and some other Christian Churches. Be clear about what Catholic teaching contains.

Summary

You should now know that the Church teaches that death is not the end. Christians believe in resurrection and a life with God after death.

5.4 Death rites

Objectives

Explain the nature and purpose of death rites (viaticum).

Know and understand the ceremonies after the death of a person at home, at church and by the graveside.

Discussion activity

What sorts of rituals can you associate with death? Why do you think people have such rituals?

A The final journey

Key terms

Death rites: ceremonies for believers in preparation for and after death.

Viaticum: a sacrament given to a person close to death to prepare for the next life.

Because Christians believe that death is not the end but part of a journey into the next life, there are a number of **death rites** which offer a preparation for that journey and mark that it has begun.

Before death

Beliefs and teachings

My brothers and sisters, before our Lord Jesus Christ passed from this world to return to the Father, he left us the sacrament of his body and blood. When the hour comes for us to pass from this life and join him, he strengthens us with this food for our journey and comforts us by his pledge of our resurrection.

Roman Rite, no. 103

Viaticum

Viaticum is the Holy Communion given to a person who is close to death. It is a very special Eucharist. Viaticum is intended to give the dying person comfort by reminding them that Jesus' suffering and death was followed by his resurrection. It therefore gives hope for life with God after death.

As someone approaches death and may be suffering, they are living through a stage of suffering in their life, just as Jesus suffered during his last week. They may feel very close to the risen Christ at this time.

B The empty tomb recalling the Lord's Easter

Activity

How may Viaticum give Christians strength in their final hours?

■ After death

The funeral Mass

There may be three parts to the rites after the death of a person. These are:

1 Vigil

This may be at home or, in some countries, in a village hall. Keeping a vigil means keeping watch all night, as members of the family and friends watch over the coffin. Sometimes this is called a 'wake'.

2 At the church

- The coffin is placed before the altar.
- The priest welcomes everyone.
- The coffin is sprinkled with holy water as a reminder of the person's baptism and that they became a Christian through baptism during their life.
- The Mass continues in the same way as a normal Mass.
- The final commendation: at the end of Mass, after some silence, the priest again sprinkles the coffin with holy water. Some last prayers as said, asking for God to draw the person who has died to him quickly and for him to be welcomed into his eternal kingdom. God is asked to look after the dead person and prayers are offered that he or she will rest in peace.

Beliefs and teachings

Before we go our separate ways, let us take leave of our brother/sister. May our farewell express our affection for him/her; may it ease our sadness and strengthen our hope. One day we shall joyfully greet him/her again when the love of Christ, which conquers all things, destroys even death itself.

Prayer from the funeral Mass

3 At the graveside

In the Catholic Church the body may be buried or cremated. Prayers are said at the graveside again. Holy water may be sprinkled again onto the coffin. Sometimes family members and friends sprinkle water before leaving the graveside.

C *Why do so many Christian gravestones have crosses on them?*

Extension activity

Create a service leaflet for a funeral. Include practical details such as the start and finish times, and the different stages of the death rites. Think carefully about the tone of leaflet and decide what explanatory information you would wish to put in it.

AQA Examiner's tip

Make sure you can say something about each of the three parts of the funeral Mass: the vigil, at the Church and at the graveside.

Summary

You should now know that the Catholic Church takes part in death rites to celebrate the Christian belief in life after death.

The sanctity of human life

What is meant by the sanctity of human life

Many Christians believe that human life is sacred. It has sanctity. This means that:

- Every individual human life is precious and has a special value beyond all price. It cannot be bargained away, ignored or sacrificed for some other good.

- As a result, human beings should not be sacrificed for a result. The deliberate taking of a human life is evil and cannot be justified except in extraordinary circumstances (such as for the defence of other human life in war).

As a result, the life of every human individual is to be respected. Life should not be taken by another human being; only God has the right to take life. However in protecting life, it may be necessary to use force against another who is a threat. Treating life as sacred may include self-defence at the individual level, or in the case of a just war, the protection of the innocent.

A 'All Human life is sacred' (Pope Paul VI, Humanae Vitae)

> *Man [is] the living image of God.*
>
> *Life is entrusted to man as a treasure which must not be squandered.*
>
> *Every human person has 'incomparable value'.*
>
> Pope John Paul II

Why do Christians believe that human beings are sacred and what are the consequences?

B

Belief	Consequence
Every human being is made in the image and likeness of God (Genesis 1:26). There is something of God in each human person.	Ending a human life is killing a God-like creature, destroying something of the image of God.
Every human life has a divine destiny. God has an intention for every human being, a purpose for them which he has decided.	Human beings must not interrupt God's purpose by taking life.
Human beings have the ability to make moral decisions. They can freely do good out of love which makes them special among all other living creatures.	By taking a life, the good possible actions of a loving, morally good, Christ-like person are ended.
Christ became human and showed the possibility of perfection that human beings can seek.	When a human life is taken, the chance of becoming more perfect and Christ-like in this world is taken away.

Activity

1 Think about the following people: a baby, an elderly person, a pregnant mother, a murderer, a severely disabled man.

a Are all their lives equally sacred? Are they equally special?

b Are some more deserving than others?

c Choose two of these people and apply the ways in which human beings are sacred to them. For instance perhaps a pregnant mother in some way is in the image of God because she is bringing new life to the world, just as all life comes from God.

C

Threats to the sanctity of life

The Church teaches that there are many threats to the sanctity of human life. These include:

- the direct taking of life: murder, genocide, abortion, euthanasia, suicide
- the violation of the human person: assault, mutilation, torture of the body or mind, forcing someone to do something against their will
- whatever denies human dignity: subhuman living conditions, cruel or unreasonable imprisonment, deportation (sending a person away to another country), slavery, prostitution, bad working conditions (where people are used as objects to get gain rather than as free and responsible persons).

These are all evil because they:

- poison human society
- cause unnecessary suffering
- harm those who practise them as well as those who suffer from the injury
- show dishonour to God who created all human lives.

Taken from the Pastoral Constitution on the Church in the Modern World Gaudium et Spes, 27

Christian duty to protect life

According to the teaching of the Catholic Church, Christians must defend and promote human beings' highest right, the right to life. They must challenge these evils and bring about a change in culture and society.

This belief is based on important biblical teachings:

- 'You shall not commit murder'.
- 'You shall love your neighbour as yourself' (Luke 10:27).
- 'If you would enter [eternal] life, keep the commandments' (Matthew 19:17).

Activity

2 How can it be argued that a murderer does harm to him/herself as well as the murdered victim?

AQA Examiner's tip

You should be able to make links between the belief that life is sacred, Bible texts and several moral issues.

Activities

3 What are the different threats to human life, according to Catholic teaching?

4 Take three examples from the first bulleted list and suggest how they threaten human life.

5 Suggest some Biblical teachings on which the Church's belief that humans have a duty to protect life is based.

Extension activity

How does the story of Cain and Abel show how human beings can abandon their human moral responsibility?

Summary

You should now understand that Christians believe in the sanctity of human life. The Catholic Church teaches that Christians have a duty to protect life and change society for the better.

5.6 Abortion: part 1

Discussion activities

1. Why is it that the discovery of unborn life brings joy to some, and fear to others?
2. When does human life begin? Give reasons for your answer.
3. What is the difference between taking the life of a newborn baby and taking the life of an unborn baby?

What is abortion?

Abortion is a serious and sensitive issue that has become increasingly important in the last fifty years, as abortions have become safer, legal and easier for women to get in the UK. A spontaneous abortion, more commonly known as a miscarriage, is when the foetus is expelled from the womb. Up to 50 per cent of pregnancies lead to miscarriage. Miscarriage is not the kind of abortion which is going to be discussed in this chapter because it occurs naturally and not as a result of choice.

Abortion, is the deliberate termination of an unborn baby usually through a medical procedure.

In the UK abortion was legalised by the 1967 Abortion Act. Before 1967 there were as many as 200,000 backstreet abortions, that is, illegal abortions often performed by unqualified people. As a result, many women became infertile after operations went wrong, and some died.

In the UK in 2005 there were 181,600 abortions. Many women come to Britain seeking abortion from countries where abortion is illegal. In UK law abortions are legal if:

- two doctors agree that it should be done
- the point of viability (when the baby can live outside the womb) has not been reached – currently given as 24 weeks
- continuing the pregnancy would be a greater risk to the mother of other children than terminating the pregnancy
- it will prevent permanent physical or psychological harm to the mother
- there is a significant risk or certainty that the baby will be born with disabilities.

In practice, if a woman wants to have an abortion and the baby is less than 24 weeks then abortions are granted on demand. In the National Health Service women may have to wait some days or weeks before the abortion can take place, but private clinics can offer 'same day' services for a fee.

Objectives

Define abortion and explain the UK law on abortion.

Explain the developmental stages of an unborn baby.

Suggest reasons why some women have abortions.

Key terms

Abortion: the deliberate termination (ending) of a pregnancy, usually before the foetus is twenty-four weeks old. Roman Catholics see this as wrong in all circumstances.

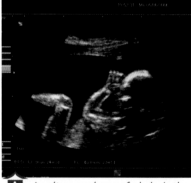

A An ultrasound scan of a baby in the mother's womb

Activity

1. Look at Diagram **B** on page 103. Why might some people argue that some of these reasons are more morally justifiable than others? Explain your answer.

Fear of parents' reaction, when the mother is a teenager

Because having the baby would interfere with the career or lifestyle of a person

When a child is not desired because the pregnancy is a result of a casual sexual encounter

Why do women have abortions?

When the life of the mother is threatened by a medical condition

Because a medical abnormality in the unborn child has been detected

Because the pregnancy is the result of rape or incest

D   *Many young women with an unplanned pregnancy are faced with a difficult choice. How can Christians support women in these situations?*

   B   *Why do women have abortions?*

Activities

2   Using Table C, decide at what point you think a foetus should have the right to life and not to be aborted? Justify your decision and compare with others in your group. If you have different views, try to explore what lies behind those differences.

C   Foetal timeline

Day 1 fertilisation	The unique genetic blueprint for the whole human being is formed
2 weeks	Primitive streak is evident (forerunner to the spine and brain)
3 weeks	The heart starts beating
6 weeks	Brainwaves are detected
8 weeks	Kicking begins (though may not be felt until later)
9 weeks	Head movement
11 weeks	Main body systems are functioning, grasping, yawning, feeling and smelling
20 weeks	Can recognise mother's voice
21 weeks	A few babies born at this point survive
24 weeks	Many babies born at this point survive
28 weeks	Baby is breathing amniotic fluid, moves and kicks
34 weeks	Baby is opening and closing eyes and soon after can see the difference between light and darkness
38–40 weeks	Birth

3   What is the UK law on abortion?

4   Why do women have abortions?

5   What is your view on abortion? Give reasons for your answer.

AQA   *Examiner's tip*

Although you do not need to learn the table, you do need to know about the main developments in early human life to explain Christian responses to abortion.

Summary

You should now know that abortion is the deliberate termination of an unborn human life by medical process. There are a number of reasons why a woman may have an abortion and different views on the point at which a foetus has a right to life.

5.7 Abortion: part 2

◼ Different responses to abortion

Arguments for abortion

Some groups of people argue in favour of legalised abortion: they are often called 'pro-choice' groups. They argue as follows:

- women have the right to choose what happens to their body
- women need these rights so they have the freedom to live independent and professional lives
- without legalised abortion, there would be a rise in backstreet abortions leading to many deaths among women
- some women may be unable, either physically or mentally, to care for a baby, or go through with the pregnancy. To do so would harm them and could endanger others.

Arguments against abortion

Opponents of abortion suggest that:

- every human being has a right to life
- there is no line that you can draw, such as 24 weeks, and say that on one side there is a human being and on the other side there isn't
- a person's unique genetic information exists from the beginning of human life – therefore they are an individual and have a right to life.

The view of the Catholic Church

The Catholic Church has always opposed abortion. There are some biblical teachings which are used to argue against abortion including the commandment 'do not kill,' and Jeremiah 1:5 'Before I formed you in the womb I knew you, before you were born I set you apart.'

The Catholic Church teaches that, from the moment of conception, a human life is created in the eyes of God. All human rights flow from the right to life. If you undermine the right to life, all rights are undermined.

The Catholic Church expects that:

- Catholic medical workers do not participate in abortions
- Catholics do not have abortions or support someone in having an abortion.

Other Christian responses

Some Christians argue that in exceptional circumstances, such as rape or where the mother's life is threatened, abortion can be justified as the lesser of two evils.

Objectives

Consider the arguments for and against abortion.

Consider Catholic teaching against abortion and alternatives to abortion.

Explore Christian responses to Church teaching on abortion.

Discussion activities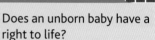

1. Does an unborn baby have a right to life?
2. Does a mother have the right to stop her reproductive system?

Beliefs and teachings

Life must be protected with the utmost care from the moment of conception. Abortion and infanticide are abominable crimes.

Gaudium Et Spes

'Centuries ago, a young pregnant woman set out on a journey. She was probably nervous and scared, because her pregnancy was unexpected, scandalous, and mysterious. The young women arrived at her cousin's home, where she hoped she would find welcome and understanding. And she was welcomed – not only by her cousin, but by another who "leapt in her (cousin's) womb" with joy. The first person to rejoice in the presence of Jesus was an unborn child.'

(from a leaflet promoting Catholic teaching on abortion and alternatives to abortion)

Alternatives to abortion

There are many ways in which people considering abortion may be helped to have the baby. The Church community can provide direct social and financial support. In cases where a teenager is involved and there are family difficulties, the Church can counsel parents or the young mother-to-be and bring the sides together. The Church community can accept and welcome single Catholic mothers fully into Parish life. In some cases the Church can help to provide temporary fostering of the child if the mother is unable to care for the child at that time, or help arrange an adoption, in extreme cases where the mother cannot care for and love the child.

The impact of the Church's teaching on abortion

Catholics respond to the Church's teachings on abortion in a number of ways. They may:

- pray for all pregnant women, especially those struggling with a difficult decision
- pray for unborn children
- support charities which campaign for the rights of the unborn
- volunteer for programmes which support single and teenage mothers
- be aware of political parties' positions on this issue and encouraging his or her local MP to represent Christian concerns in Parliament.

The Catholic Church also reminds Christians about the Gospel message of loving forgiveness. Counselling and support must be offered to women who have had abortions. They must be helped to seek reconciliation with God and should be treated with compassion.

Beliefs and teachings

The Church of England combines strong opposition to abortion with a recognition that there can be – strictly limited – conditions under which it may be morally preferable to any available alternative.

General Synod

A   *An expectant mother looks at a picture of her unborn child*

Activities

1   Why is the Catholic Church opposed to abortion?
2   For what reasons might some women feel they simply cannot go through with a pregnancy?
3   What are the alternatives to abortion?
4   Considering all of the information on these pages, identify what you consider to be the four strongest arguments against abortion and the four strongest arguments in favour of abortion. Discuss these with a partner and then come to a decision yourself on the issue. Explain your decision.

Summary

You should now know that there are many arguments for and against abortion. Catholic teaching is clearly opposed to abortion.

AQA   Examiner's tip

Make sure you can link the attitudes towards abortion with specific Christian teachings.

Contraception

Contraception in Britain

In contemporary British society the use of artificial **contraception** to prevent pregnancy is widespread. This is usually either through the use of a contraceptive pill or a condom. The availability of contraception is seen as one way in which women can lead working lives and be more independent than in the past.

Contraception has made casual sex more possible than before but means there is a greater risk from sexually transmitted diseases and unwanted pregnancy. This is what the media and government advice about contraception has in mind.

Though contraception is widely available, Britain has the highest rate of teenage pregnancy in Europe.

Catholic teaching on contraception

The Catholic Church, however, teaches that sexual relationships should only exist within a marriage. This means that its view of contraception is connected with its belief about marriage. The Church teaches that lovemaking is both a uniting and a reproductive act, that is it unites the couple and has the possibility of reproducing new life. It teaches that both aspects of lovemaking should be present.

Contraception raises questions about the openness and completeness of love expressed in love making. Contraception means there is no life to be held sacred, and yet the Church teaches that even the possibility of creating life is sacred. It is a gift of marriage and one of the purposes of lovemaking.

Natural family planning, or natural contraception

The Catholic Church promotes natural family planning, or natural contraception which are methods given by God to help to a couple plan their family. They should not be used to remove fully the possibility of creating new life at any time from their marriage. The methods are:

- agreeing not to make love
- the rhythm method. Getting to know the woman's menstrual cycle, and the times when she cannot conceive and making love in these times
- body function methods. Getting to know mucous patterns and temperatures to find out when the chance of fertilisation is low and making love in these times.

Artificial contraception and emergency of contraception

Artificial contraception

Artificial contraception means forms of contraception which act as a barrier to new life. For example the condom, which is a physical barrier, preventing sperm from reaching the egg, and the contraceptive pill, a chemical barrier preventing the woman from ovulating each month.

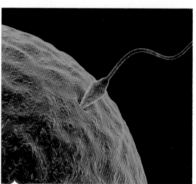

A *Being open to the possibility of new life is one of the purposes of lovemaking*

Emergency contraception

Emergency contraception is also known as the morning after pill. It is a type of artificial contraception taken up to three days after sex. It stops the production of an egg and stops eggs from sticking to the side of the womb. In this case the egg may have been fertilised.

Views of the Church

The Church teaches that the use of both artificial and emergency contraception is a sin because:

- they prevent the possibility of new life, part of the purpose of making love
- they mean the couple are holding something back when they make love
- in addition, in the case of emergency contraception, there is a grave possibility that the egg has been fertilised in which case emergency contraception results in the termination of a human life.

Not making love is obviously 100 per cent reliable, artificial forms of contraception if used properly are nearly 100 per cent reliable and natural forms of contraception if used properly are 85–98 per cent effective.

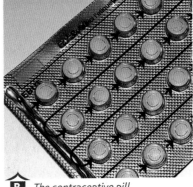

B *The contraceptive pill*

Christian debate about contraception

There is a great deal of debate about this issue. Some Christians argue that personal situations can make this teaching very difficult, for instance if one partner has HIV/AIDS. It is sometimes said that limiting the number of children is a responsible thing to do. Some believe that the issue of contraception should be left to individual conscience. The Church teaches that couples who find the teaching too difficult should examine it carefully and pray about it. In following their conscience some Catholics find themselves going against the Church's teaching.

Activities

1   Define natural contraception, artificial contraception and emergency contraception.

2   What is the Catholic Church's teaching on:

a   natural contraception

b   artificial contraception

c   emergency contraception?

3   What advice does the Church give to people who are finding the teaching difficult to follow? Why do you think it gives such advice?

4   What arguments might some Christians put forward against the Church's teaching?

AQA *Examiner's tip*

Remember that the Catholic Church teaches that artificial contraception is wrong, but natural forms of contraception are acceptable.

Summary

You should now understand that there is much debate amongst Christians about the use of contraception. The Roman Catholic Church teaches that the use of artificial contraception is wrong.

5.9 In vitro fertilisation

Discussion activities

1. Why does not being able to have children cause so much suffering?
2. Do people have a right to have children or are they a gift that people may be blessed to receive?

Most couples expect to be able to have children and are able to. However 1 in 7 couples cannot after a year of trying. Some fertility problems can be treated but others are more difficult to overcome. In some cases a couple cannot have children naturally.

What is IVF?

IVF (in vitro fertilisation) is a medical procedure for infertile couples. The first 'test tube baby' was Louise Brown, born in 1978. Around 6,000 babies a year are now born using IVF. In IVF, a woman's ovaries are stimulated to produce multiple eggs. Several eggs are fertilised with her partner's sperm making embryos. These are placed in the mother's womb while others are frozen for use later if needed. If they are not used they are usually destroyed.

In some cases **donor** sperm or ovum is used, which means that the sperm or ovum is given by a third person. Sometimes fertilised eggs are placed inside a **surrogate mothers**, who becomes pregnant and gives birth for the couple.

IVF is expensive, about £2,000 for a treatment, and is paid for by the government rather than the couple themselves. Around 15 per cent of attempts are successful.

Objectives

Explore what IVF is and suggest why couples might use it.

Identity some moral questions involved in IVF and arguments for and against it.

Examine Catholic teachings on IVF and other Christian responses.

Key terms

In vitro fertilisation (IVF): A scientific method of making a woman pregnant, which does not involve sex. Conception occurs via sperm and egg being placed in a test tube.

Donor: another person who donates sperm or ovum for a couple who are infertile.

Surrogate mother: a women who carries and gives birth to a child of another couple.

Infertility: an inability to conceive a child naturally.

Case study

Andrew and Sarah

Andrew and Sarah are a married couple. Both wife and husband felt that having children was part of their purpose in life. After two years of trying to become pregnant, a doctor told them that they could not do so naturally. This was a devastating blow to the couple. They had both always wished for a large family and often talked about the children they would have. Both Andrew and Sarah suffered from depression and great sadness as a result of their **infertility**.

After several years, Andrew and Sarah attempted IVF using Sarah's eggs and Andrew's sperm. Fertilised embryos were place in Sarah's womb and she became pregnant with twins. She later gave birth to two healthy baby boys. Andrew, Sarah and their children now enjoy a happy family life.

A *Embryologist freezing embryos for storage*

Moral dilemmas surrounding IVF

Arguments for IVF

Those who support IVF argue that:

- infertility is an illness that can cause sadness and depression. Those suffering from infertility should receive treatment as with any other illness
- all couples should have a right to try for children. For some, IVF is the only way.

Arguments against IVF

The Catholic Church opposes IVF because it:

- can lead to the destruction of new life:
  - frozen embryos which are stored but never used are usually destroyed
  - several embryos are implanted to make it more likely that there will be a successful pregnancy. If more than one of the embryos survives, this leads to multiple births (for example twins, triplets). The couple may then choose to remove some of the embryos to leave only one. This is abortion. However, some people choose to do this because it increases the chances that the remaining embryo will survive
- separates the creation of new life (reproduction) from the intimate uniting act of sex. The Church teaches that sex should be both a loving encounter and an opportunity for new life and these two purposes must not be separated
- brings others into the process: the medical experts and possibly a donor or a surrogate mother. This challenges the exclusiveness of the marriage
- encourages the idea that there is a right to have children, forgetting they are a gift
- is a costly method and has a low success rate
- should not be the last resort. There are many children in need of adoption. Couples could put themselves forward to adopt.

Other Christian responses

Some Christians may argue that if no embryos are destroyed then there is nothing wrong with IVF. It is overcoming an illness, just as Jesus brought healing to many others. God asked human beings to have children, and this is simply using God-given knowledge (science) to fulfil God's plan.

Alternatives to IVF

The Church realises that it can be very sad for couples who cannot conceive. There are other forms of fertility treatment which do not involve the separation of reproduction from the uniting loving act in sex, and which do not lead to the destruction of embryos. There are fertility drugs and other methods which can help couples conceive, although not all couples can conceive in these other ways.

Activities

1. What is IVF?
2. Why might a couple want to have IVF?
3. What are the moral issues involved in IVF?
4. What does the Catholic Church teach about IVF?
5. Consider the arguments for and against, and the alternatives to IVF and different Christian responses:
   a. Identity the strongest argument for and against IVF.
   b. Explain why you think they are strong.
   c. Decide what you think and explain why.

Summary

You should now know that there are many arguments for and against the use of IVF, as well as many moral dilemmas. The Roman Catholic Church opposes IVF.

5.10 Euthanasia

What is euthanasia?

Many people suffer at their end of their lives. They may become disabled physically or mentally, and may feel a lot of pain. It can be distressing for friends and family.

Euthanasia is often defined as the act of killing someone painlessly, especially to relieve suffering from an incurable illness. It can be done actively, which means that something is done to the person to end their life, such as giving them a lethal injection. It can also be done passively, meaning that something necessary for life is not given to the person, for instance not giving them food or water. The word euthanasia means an 'easy or good death'. It is sometimes called mercy killing.

Kinds of euthanasia

- **Voluntary euthanasia**: where the person suffering has asked for or consented to euthanasia.
- **Non-voluntary euthanasia**: euthanasia where the person's consent cannot be given, because, for instance, they are in a coma.
- **Involuntary euthanasia**: this is the killing of a person against their will for some social or medical justification. For instance the Nazis killed disabled people because they were thought to be of no 'use'.

Laws about euthanasia in the UK and throughout the world

Euthanasia is against the law in the UK and in most parts of the world but the UK law allows doctors to:

- give a powerful painkiller to a terminally ill patient who is suffering even if, as a secondary affect, the person dies sooner
- withdraw medical treatment if they judge that recovery is not possible. This may involve turning off a life support machine. In some cases it has been possible to withdraw food and water.

In 2006 the Assisted Dying Bill was defeated in the House of Lords. It would have allowed terminally ill people to be helped to die.

A

Arguments for euthanasia	**Mercy**: for compassionate reasons, animals' lives are ended when their suffering becomes too great – why not humans? Some Christians suggest that showing mercy in this way can be showing love.
	Freedom: humans should have the right to choose the time and nature of their own death.
	Quality of life: if a person is suffering terribly and no cure or relief is possible then the quality of their life may be very poor.
	The person may wish to be remembered as the person they always have been – they do not wish to make their family suffer seeing pain and suffering coming to someone they love.
Catholic teachings on euthanasia	Every life is sacred and valuable, and should not be taken. God has a divine purpose for every single person
	'Life is always a good' (Pope John Paul II). Even though a person may be suffering it is possible that, in the mystery of suffering, some goodness may come in the situation, such as in the love shown the person by others, the care given by doctors and nurses. Humans are stewards of their lives, not owners of them – God should be the only one to take away life.
	Suffering is a mystery, and in suffering a person comes close to the suffering of the crucified Christ (Phillippians 3:10; 1 Peter 2:21), so there is a purpose to suffering.
	The Church acknowledges that:
	▪ someone close to death may be given powerful painkillers which also shorten the person's life ▪ attempts to save a life might simply be trying to ignore the inevitability of death.
	Both of these things are not euthanasia and are not considered wrong.
Biblical teachings linked to euthanasia	It is God who chooses the time of our death: 'I put to death and bring to life' (Deuteronomy 32:39).
	The commandment opposes killing: 'Do not kill' and lists no exceptions.
	Jesus came to heal people not to kill them.
	Suffering is part of Christian discipleship '… Christ suffered for you, leaving you an example, that you should follow in his steps.' (1 Peter 2:21).

Alternatives to euthanasia

The hospice movement is an example of a different, Christian response to the terminally ill. There experts caring for people and providing pain relief can look after those nearing the end of their life in comfortable warm surroundings. Many churches and church schools support local hospices by fundraising, sending volunteers to work there and arranging visits, such as carol concerts at Christmas.

B   *How do the work of hospices reflect Christian beliefs?*

Activities

3   Consider the arguments for and against euthanasia. Of the arguments given, which is the strongest argument for euthanasia and why?

4   How are the biblical teachings connected with Catholic teachings?

5   Explain Christian arguments in favour of euthanasia.

AQA   Examiner's tip

Remember that for some Christians the sanctity of life means life should be worth living.

Summary

You should now understand that there are many arguments for and against euthanasia. The Roman Catholic Church opposes euthanasia.

5

Christian healing – summary

For the examination you should now be able to:

✔ explain the phrase 'anointing the sick'

✔ explain the Christian beliefs about suffering and healing

✔ outline the Rite of the Anointing of the Sick and explain the symbolism

✔ explain the Christian beliefs about death and life after death and the death rites in the Roman Catholic tradition

✔ explain the terms sanctity of life, abortion and euthanasia

✔ explain the legal situation regarding abortion and euthanasia and why people sometimes seek abortion and euthanasia

✔ outline and explain arguments for and against abortion and euthanasia

✔ explain Catholic teaching and how Christians might respond to Catholic teachings on abortion and euthanasia

✔ explain the terms relating to contraception and in vitro fertilisation (IVF)

✔ outline the reasons why people use contraception and why some people seek fertility treatments using IVF, donor sperm/ovum and surrogate mothers

✔ explain Catholic teaching on contraception and IVF

✔ Study Roman Catholic beliefs and attitudes to these issues relating to protecting, respecting, and preserving human life.

Sample answer

1 Write an answer to the following exam question.

'Euthanasia can be the most loving thing for someone who is terminally ill'

Do you agree? Give reasons for your answer, showing that you have thought about more than one point of view. Refer to Roman Catholic teaching in your answer. *(6 marks)*

2 Read the following sample answer:

> If someone is terminally ill and the pain that they are suffering is too much for them to bear then it might be more loving for them to be allowed to die using a lethal injection if they want to. Usually we should try to heal the sick but when nothing can be done it is better for them to have a

> good death. However some Christians think that this is wrong because it is murder. The Bible says do not kill. The Catholic Church teaches that Christians should never take life like this because all life is sacred. I think that God does not want people to suffer and so euthanasia can be the best thing for someone.

3 With a partner, discuss the sample answer. Do you think that there are other things that the student could have included in the answer?

4 What mark would you give this answer out of 6? Look at the mark scheme in the Introduction on page 7 (AO2). What are the reasons for the mark you have given?

AQA Examination-style questions

1 Look at the photograph and answer the following questions.

(a) What is meant by the word euthanasia?   *(2 marks)*

(b) Explain why the Roman Catholic Church is opposed to the use of artificial contraception.   *(4 marks)*

(c) Outline the rite of the anointing of the sick.   *(6 marks)*

(d) 'A Christian should not have or help with an abortion'
     Do you agree? Give reasons for your answer, showing that you have thought about more than one point of view. Refer to Roman Catholic teaching in your answer.   *(6 marks)*

AQA
Examiner's tip
Remember when explaining the teaching of the Roman Catholic Church, you can refer to bible sayings, as well as teachings from the catechism, or statement by religious leaders. Try to link these sources of the teachings with the moral response to show how one leads to the other.

6 Christian responses to global issues

6.1 Christian duty towards the poor and those in need

▣ The dignity of the human person

Why do people matter?

'The glory of God is a person fully alive' (St Irenaeus). The Roman Catholic Church teaches that every single human being has dignity. The human person is a sacred, unique being, created by God and in His image. The human person has the amazing potential of freely choosing to love others and love God. The human person has an eternal destiny to be with God. God reveals himself on earth through human beings.

A single human family

The Bible commands Christians to love their **neighbour** as themselves. Loving your neighbour includes actively caring for those in need. Christians must 'consider every neighbour without exception as another self, taking into account first of all his life and the means necessary for living it with dignity' (Gaudium et Spes 27 (1966)). Christians must recognise the human dignity of all men and women.

All human beings share in God's image and share being created by God. They belong to one family so must:

- work for the common good
- not be divided by material wealth. God has given all humanity the world with all its resources to be shared, not for some to be rich while others live in poverty.

A *One human family*

Activities

1. What do you think it might mean to say that human beings should be treated with dignity?
2. Can you think of examples where people are living in humiliating conditions or situations?
3. In what ways do you think that the human family is divided?
4. Why do you think the Catholic Church teaches that inequalities in resources are sinful?

The mission of love: justice, peace and reconciliation in the world

According to the Gospel:

- Jesus was sent to 'preach the good news to the poor.' (Luke 4:1).
- The poor are blessed and the kingdom of heaven is theirs (see Matthew 5:3).
- The poor are waiting for justice (see Luke 1:17).

The Church speaks to all people and calls them to Christ and the salvation and freedom that he offers. Christians have a duty to attend to the demands of justice and peace for God loves the world, the whole human family. It is an urgent mission.

The preferential option for the poor

A moral test for society is how it treats the most vulnerable within it. The Catholic Church has a 'preferential option for the poor'. This means that the Church teaches the poor have the strongest right to our help.

Charity could be seen as giving a little bit of wealth to others because we are kind and generous. Others see it differently. The rich have benefited greatly from the wealth that was meant for all. Their share is too large.

> 66 When we Christians make Jesus Christ the centre of our thoughts, we do not turn away from people and their needs ... The poor of the world are your brothers and sisters in Christ. You must never be content to leave them just the crumbs from the feast. You must take of your substance, and not just of your abundance, in order to help them. 99
>
> John Paul II Speech in Yankee Stadium, 1979

B *Our brothers and sisters?*

Beliefs and teachings

A modern pope, Pope John Paul II (1920–2005), wrote the following:

> How can it be that even today there are still people dying of hunger? Condemned to illiteracy? Lacking the most basic medical care? Without a roof over their head? ... Christians must learn to make their act of faith in Christ by discerning his voice in the cry for help that rises from this world of poverty.
>
> Pope John Paul II Apostolic Letter Novo Millenio Inuento 50–51: AAS 93 (2001) 303–4

Activities

5   'Christians in rich countries should be worried!' Do you agree? Give reasons for your answer.

6   If you were a Christian, should you go to school tomorrow or go out into the world to help those in need? Prepare two different arguments.

7   Suggest why thinking about others as brothers or sisters might change the way Christians treat them?

AQA *Examiner's tip*

Make sure you can link Jesus' teachings about the poor with Catholic responses to the poor.

Summary

You should now understand Christians have a responsibility to do good and to help the poor and those in need out of obedience to Jesus and respect for each other.

Matthew 25:31–46

This text is often described as a parable, a story with one or more meanings. It is also a vision of the end of time with many messages about the kind of faith that Christianity is.

Beliefs and teachings

...Then the King will say to those on his right, "Come, you who are blessed by my Father; take your inheritance, the kingdom prepared for you since the creation of the world. For I was hungry and you gave me something to eat, I was thirsty and you gave me something to drink, I was a stranger and you invited me in, I needed clothes and you clothed me, I was sick and you looked after me, I was in prison and you came to visit me." Then the righteous will answer him, "Lord, when did we see you hungry and feed you, or thirsty and give you something to drink? When did we see you a stranger and invite you in, or needing clothes and clothe you? When did we see you sick or in prison and go to visit you?" The King will reply, "I tell you the truth, whatever you did for one of the least of these brothers of mine, you did for me." Then he will say to those on his left, "Depart from me, you who are cursed, into the eternal fire prepared for the devil and his angels. For I was hungry and you gave me nothing to eat, I was thirsty and you gave me nothing to drink, I was a stranger and you did not invite me in, I needed clothes and you did not clothe me, I was sick and in prison and you did not look after me." They also will answer, "Lord, when did we see you hungry or thirsty or a stranger or needing clothes or sick or in prison, and did not help you?" He will reply, "I tell you the truth, whatever you did not do for one of the least of these, you did not do for me." Then they will go away to eternal punishment, but the righteous to eternal life.

Matthew 25:34–46

AQA *Examiner's tip*

Make sure you know this parable and how Christians use it when responding to the poor.

Extension activity

Read Deuteronomy 24:17–21, Isaiah 58:9–10, Luke 12:16–21, Luke 16:19–31, Acts 4:34–37, John 10:10, Luke 12:33–34. Write a short paragraph on what each of these passages adds to your understanding of Matthew 25:31–46.

Interpreting the text

A religion of loving kindness

Matthew 25:31–46 is a powerful text. Christians have a duty to love their neighbour. This is at the heart of what it means to be Christian. Loving Christ means serving others, especially the needy.

A *Does she have dignity?*

B *Are we indifferent?*

C *New arrivals*

The works of mercy

The Parable of the Sheep and the Goats shows ways Christians can demonstrate practical loving kindness:

- visiting and looking after the sick
- welcoming the strangers in society
- providing for those who are hungry and thirsty
- clothing and respecting those who have lost everything, who are stripped of dignity (naked)
- visiting and attending to the needs of those who are in prison.

Christian moral responsibility

Christians are bound then to care for those in need out of:

- obedience to Jesus
- respect for human beings
- and in a response to the love of God shown to human beings through Jesus.

St John Chrysostom (4th century) was an important early father of the Church whose teaching guides Christians today.

D   *Christ was marginalised and crucified*

> 66 *Consider that Christ is that tramp who comes in need of a night's lodging. You turn him away and then start laying rugs on the floor, draping the walls, hanging lamps on silver chains on the columns. … look after the poor first … adorn your house if you will, but do not forget your brothers in distress.* 99
>
> *Homily,* 5.4

St Basil was an influential 4th-century monk known for his care of the poor and underprivileged.

> 66 *What keeps you from giving now? Isn't the poor man there? … The command is clear; the hungry man is dying now, the naked man is freezing now, the man in debt is beaten now, and you want to wait until tomorrow? … If everyone took only what he needed and gave the rest to those in need, there would be no such thing as rich and poor… You do wrong to everyone you could help, but fail to help.* 99
>
> St Basil 4th century AD

Activities

1. Why might wealthy Christians in richer countries feel challenged by these extracts?
2. Using information from these two pages, devise a flow diagram illustrating how beliefs about human dignity and the human family lead to certain attitudes to the poor.
3. Take two powerful phrases from Matthew 23:31–46 and think of as many different specific ways you can illustrate each of the phrases. You could try to draw them or describe them.
4. 'I have hardly got enough money to make ends meet myself, to go about giving away what little I have to others.' Try to make a Christian argument for or against this point of view.

Summary

You should now understand that Christians can receive many messages from The Parable of the Sheep and the Goats showing how Christian faith can be understood and how Christians can serve others.

A world divided by wealth

1   The world is filled with great resources and great inequalities. Consider these three quotations:

a   'The earth has enough for everyone's need, but not enough for everyone's greed' (Mahatma Gandhi).

b   'Poverty is like punishment for a crime you didn't commit' (Eli Khamarov).

c   'Every social group must take account of the needs and legitimate aspirations of other groups, and even of the general welfare of the entire human family' (Catholic Church, Gaudium et Spes, The Church and the Modern World, 1965:26).

Suggest in your own words what each quotation means and decide whether you agree with it or not.

What is poverty?

Each day 40,000 children starve to death. Many are born into poverty and many are born into situations where life is short. Extreme poverty has been defined as living on less than one dollar a day, which means that people cannot meet basic needs for survival, such as food, water, clothing, shelter, sanitation, education and health care. One in five of the world's population live in extreme poverty.

How are the world's resources distributed?

The resources of the world are not evenly shared. In Europe and Central Asia, 3.5 per cent of people live in extreme poverty while in Sub-Saharan Africa the figure is 38.5 per cent. Poorer countries are known as **less economically developed (LED)**. A recent report found that the richest 1 per cent of people own 40 per cent of the world's wealth while 50 per cent of the world's adults own just 1 per cent of the world's wealth. Very few people have most of the world's wealth and very many people have virtually none of it.

> 66 *God has made the earth and all that it contains for all to share. The earth's goods must be divided fairly and this right of everyone to a just share comes first. All other rights must help, not block, this basic right of every human being.* 99
>
> Pope Paul VI, Populorum Pregresso

How are the lives of the rich and the poor different?

Five basic needs

Throughout the world there are wide differences between rich and poor but all human beings have five basic needs.

Recall and explain what is meant by extreme poverty.

Identify specific differences between rich and poor.

Evaluate whether the world distribution of wealth is fair.

Less economically developed (LED): poorer countries.

1   Apply the distribution of the world's resources to something in your school, home or community. For instance school lunches: How would you feel if half of your class had to share one half of one lunch portion, while one person got to eat half of the total class's lunch (15 if you are in class of 30)? Could such an arrangement be justified?

2   Translate the figures for wealth distribution into an image, chart or diagram illustrating the differences.

A   *Women and girls frequently have to carry water long distances meaning they are unable to go to school or have a profession*

The following table compares the experience of rich and poor countries.

B

Need	Rich world	Poor world
Food	■ Food is relatively cheap, varied and easy to come by. ■ Overeating is a cause of many health problems for people in developed countries.	■ Food is scarce, difficult to come by and expensive. ■ Malnutrition is common, leading to disease.
Water	■ Water is taken for granted. ■ Even in times of water shortage it is rarely unavailable on tap. ■ People feel frustrated if they are not allowed to water their flowerbeds using a hosepipe.	■ 1.2 billion people do not have access to safe drinking water and 2.6 billion do not have access to sanitation causing 2 million child deaths each year. ■ Millions of women and girls spend hours collecting and carrying water.
Education	■ Primary and secondary education is free and all have access to education. ■ The more highly educated you are the more highly paid job you are likely to end up doing.	■ 855 million people are functionally illiterate and 73 million children receive no primary education.
	The longer children spend in education, the lower the rate of infact mortality.	
Health	■ In the UK fewer than five children out of every thousand born die before their first birthday. ■ In the UK there is free access to local GPs and hospitals and drugs and other treatments are subsidised (part paid for out of taxation) or free for children, the elderly, pregnant mothers and those on low incomes.	■ In parts of India 15 in every thousand children die before their first birthday. ■ In many poorer countries hospital provision is poor, so that travel to hospital may take days leading to a loss of earnings. Drug treatments must be paid for and so treatable diseases get worse.
	Sometimes particular groups are badly affected within rich countries. In the USA African-American mothers are twice as likely to lose their child before the first birthday as white American mothers.	
Work	■ More people have jobs and those jobs usually involve higher skill levels and a higher income as a result. ■ Working conditions are monitored and controlled to ensure people are not mistreated or forced to work in dangerous conditions. ■ In times of unemployment there is financial support and opportunities for training to get back into work.	■ Many people have low-paid and low-skilled jobs which offer few opportunities to grow and flourish and barely enough to live on if at all. ■ Working conditions are less regulated so people may have very long days with little appropriate protection or consideration of worker safety. ■ In times of unemployment there is little or no support or opportunities for training, leaving the workers in poverty and with no sense of dignity.

Data source: UN and World Bank

Activities

3 Take one of the five basic needs in Table **B** and, working in groups, try to portray the contrast of the rich and poor world. This could be done using human sculpture, art or a very short role play.

4 Look at the quote from Pope Paul VI on page 118. In the light of this teaching, how might Catholics see the differences between rich and poor?

Summary

You should now understand that the world's wealth is unfairly divided between rich, developed countries and less economically developed countries. Many people in these countries have physical needs which are not met and have few safe and rewarding work opportunities.

AQA   *Examiner's tip*

There are many ways in which the lives of the rich and poor are different. Remember how they differ when it comes to the basic needs that humans have.

What are the causes of world poverty?

Man made or environmental?

While life in the UK is rarely interrupted by environmental disaster, other parts of the world are more prone to natural disasters, such as droughts or famine, which can cause poverty. Increasingly, however, poverty is also the result of human activity. Look at Table **A** below for some examples of the causes of **world poverty**.

A Worldwide causes of poverty

Cause	Impact
Environmental problems	Frequent natural disasters, such as droughts, destroy crops which mean whole communities are seriously weakened. Poor countries do not have the resources to be resilient to such disasters, so families go unfed, workers become weaker and more prone to disease and less fit to work when conditions change. Increasingly, natural disasters are the result of man-made pollution of the environment.
Healthcare	The lack of basic healthcare means child mortality is high, women are more likely to die in childbirth, people are still dying from preventable illnesses, and too many people die unnecessarily. And so it is very difficult for families and communities to develop economically.
Conflict	War and civil unrest use up money and other resources on arms and conflict, while health, education, agriculture, and so forth, suffer. Conflict often drives people from their homes and destroys their livelihoods, therefore they may no longer be safe and are less able to provide for themselves.
Poor leadership	Governments or rulers that are corrupt or incompetent waste resources and may make bad decisions. Countries that were relatively stable have been brought to economic collapse by corrupt rulers.
HIV/AIDS	In some countries huge numbers of people suffer from HIV and AIDS. Often the group affected are young adults – an important part of the workforce. They die young or are seriously weakened, meaning the country cannot develop.
Debt	Poor countries have in the past had to borrow large sums of money from rich countries and now have to pay back the loan rather than spend money on necessities for their people.
Trade barriers	Unfair trade rules benefit richer countries. Very poor countries are prevented from selling their produce to richer countries, or forced to compete against subsidised rich countries.

Objectives

Describe the causes of poverty.

Explain the poverty cycle using an example.

Key terms

World poverty: the idea that the majority of the world's population actually live in conditions of extreme need or hardship.

B Long-lasting drought is an environmental factor that can cause poverty

Activities

1. Devise a diagram or picture which illustrates the different causes of poverty.

2. Choose one of the causes in Table **A** and devise a flow diagram which shows how this may lead to a poverty cycle (a situation in which the person is trapped in poverty). An example based on loss of crops through a natural disaster such as drought can be seen in Diagram **B**.

An example of the poverty cycle

Poor nutrition and poor general health takes the lives of the young adult workers

The older generation of grandparents are left to look after the children and work

Less money to buy food

Hunger and poor health mean the person is less able to both care for the children and work

It is difficult to do both so not enough wealth is made from working to feed the family

 Poverty can lead to a cycle of decline (the poverty circle)

Poor government in Zimbabwe (2008)

Case study

Zimbabwe is in the southern part of Africa. The country has been independent for many years and had valuable resources and productive farms. In 2000 the Government introduced a land reform policy of taking farms from white owners and giving them to black people. However, the people given the farms were often supporters of Robert Mugabe's governing party. The farms were looted and fell into disuse. Zimbabwe now suffers from hyperinflation which means the money paid to workers quickly becomes worthless. Many people currently struggle to find enough food to feed their families. Huge numbers of people are abandoning their homes and leaving the country in search of security and help. Zimbabwe was a productive country, but has been brought to the brink of collapse by poor government.

Extension activity

Use the internet to find out about other countries affected by poverty. Find an example that is man-made and one caused by environmental diaster.

Activity

3   Examine the case study on Zimbabwe and devise a flow diagram to show the stages of decline.

Summary

You should now understand how poverty is sometimes the result of environmental, health and man-made factors which trigger a decline into poverty.

6.5 How do Christians respond to the needs of the poor overseas?

Discussion activities

1 'There's nothing we can do to change the world. The best we can hope for is to try and help those nearby.' Is this realistic or pessimistic?

2 Is our ability to make a difference greater than we sometimes think? Consider examples in your own and others' lives.

How do Christians respond to poverty?

The New Testament says 'If anyone has the world's goods and sees his brother in need, yet closes his heart against him, how does God's love abide in him? Little children, let us not love in word or speech, but in deed and truth' (John 3:17–18). Good wishes are not enough – actions and honesty are necessary. The church teaches that Christians are not spectators of society and do not live in private worlds. There is only one world and it is God's world. All have a duty to the care of the world.

Christians may believe that the wealth divisions in the world are unjust and that poverty is an evil but what can they do about it? The troubles of the world can seem hopelessly overwhelming.

Discussion activities

3 Can a person be called a good Christian if they raise a lot of money for the poor overseas but do not look after their family and friends?

4 Could a Christian be justified in leaving home to work overseas to help the very poor?

> " Love begins by taking care of the closest ones – the ones at home. "
>
> Mother Teresa

> " Do not honour Jesus here in church clothed in silk vestments and then pass him by unclothed and frozen outside "
>
> St John Chrysostom

Christian action: prayer

Christians may pray for the poor at Church and in their personal prayers. In the Bible Jesus teaches that Christians must pray with persistence. When a person prays, it may be to ask for help or for the ability to make changes. The prayer 'Make Poverty History' shows this.

Activity

1 Identify three things which this prayer commands Christians to do and suggest three practical ways in which they might do them.

Objectives

Identify and describe three different Christian responses to the poor in less developed countries.

Understand how one Roman Catholic school contributed to the 'Make Poverty History' campaign.

Evaluate the importance of caring for the poor overseas and those near to hand.

Make Poverty History

Motivate me, O Lord, to overcome
  Apathy and to embrace your
    Kingdom of justice.
      Energise me, that I may strive to

Prevent the poverty that
  Oppresses millions in Africa, and
  Vanquish the
    Evil which
      Reduces and
        Traumatises the humanity of
          Your beloved children.

Help me,
  Inform me,
    Sustain me,
      Transform me,
        Open me to my
          Responsibility to change
            Your world. Amen.

Canon Chris Chivers, Christian Aid
Connect website

A *Prayer*

Christian action: charity

Many Catholic Churches have **charities**, 'Justice and Peace' groups and other groups which work to raise money to support emergency aid and development projects overseas. Money is raised through collections at church services, fetes and other fundraising activities.

> 66 *Christ has no body on earth but yours, no hands but yours, no feet but yours. Yours are the eyes through which Christ's compassion for the world is to look out; yours are the feet with which He is to go about doing good; and yours are the hands with which He is to bless us now.* 99
>
> St Teresa of Avila

Christian action: campaigning for change

The 'Make Poverty History' campaign was established to bring about political change for the world's poor.

> **Case study**
>
> ### Message for students: make poverty history
>
> Many of you will be familiar with the idea of the white wristbands which are being sold and worn to bring attention to the plight of the poorer countries of the world. Here at St John Houghton Catholic School we are interested in playing our part in raising awareness of this subject. Many students have recently done work on Fairtrade and had guest speakers tell them about how we can become involved. As part of our active participation in this campaign, we are holding a 'Question Time' session on February 24th, during which students from Years 10 and 11 will have the opportunity to ask questions to a panel consisting of local political and religious leaders. To publicise this event, and to make the strength of our feelings known, we are proposing that on that day each pupil in the school will wear a white armband. In addition to this, we are planning to put a white band around the whole school building which will look dramatic and hopefully bring attention to the 'Make Poverty History' campaign. The BBC plans to visit the school with a film crew during the day, so look out for us on the local news. In July 2005 we are hoping to have a school presence at the G8 conference to join our voice to those of others to MAKE POVERTY HISTORY.
>
> *Adapted from Saint John Houghton Catholic School, Newsletter 2005*

Key terms

Charity: Christian action for those in need.

Discussion activity

5   In groups of three consider the different kinds of Christian activity on these pages: prayer, charity and campaigning for change. Take one of these headings each. Each member of the group must make a speech explaining why their choice is the best Christian response. Then discuss which argument you are genuinely most convinced by.

Activity

2   Identify the different activities in the newsletter which could be called a Christian response to poverty. How do you think these different activities might bring about change?

Summary

You should now know that the Church teaches that Christians should pray for the poor, be charitable towards them and work for change in the world.

AQA   *Examiner's tip*

Make sure you are able to give specific examples of Christian responses to the poor.

6.6 CAFOD and Trócaire

Faith in action

Two Catholic organisations dedicated to supporting the poorest and most marginalised throughout the world are **CAFOD** and **Trócaire**. Their activities include: educational and awareness campaigns, emergency relief, development projects, and justice and advocacy work.

Case study

CAFOD

CAFOD believes in dignity and respect for all human beings. The world's resources should be shared equally by all people, regardless of race, nationality or religion. When helping those who live in immense poverty and suffering, CAFOD responds with compassion and action. They work and pray side by side with excluded communities to provide much-needed resources and bring people independence. CAFOD defends the rights of those in need and works to change the systems that encourage poverty.

A www.cafod.org.uk

Trócaire

Trócaire believes that a just world ensures the dignity of all people. All individual have a right to have their basic needs met. Trócaire supports both long-term development projects and much needed short-term emergency relief in countries across the globe. Trócaire also works with those closer to home, as demonstrated in recent projects that inform the Irish public about ways to prevent poverty and injustice by dealing with the root causes. Trócaire works to motivate and mobilise the public to bring about global change.

B http://trocaire.org

Objectives

Know and understand the different aspects of the work of CAFOD and Trócaire.

Identify the differences between short-term disaster relief and long-term development work.

Key terms

CAFOD: Catholic Fund for Overseas Development – charity established by the Bishops of England and Wales to bring aid to less economically developed countries.

Trócaire: Irish word for mercy; charity established by the Irish bishops to help alleviate poverty in the developing world.

Educational awareness, justice and advocacy

CAFOD and Trócaire work to educate people in richer countries about the situation for people in poorer countries using leaflets, posters, books, videos and the internet to encourage awareness and fund raising in schools, churches and other community groups. Different themes and projects are selected from year to year, responding to new and ongoing emergencies.

CAFOD and Trócaire work for justice in the world and defend the rights of the poor and marginalised. They especially provide help for victims of HIV/AIDS and help women gain access to education and jobs.

Short-term aid (emergency relief)

Through local organisations throughout the world, CAFOD and Trócaire respond very quickly to sudden emergencies and disasters. Trócaire's emergency response to the Burma cyclone in 2008 has provided life-saving food supplies for 350,000 people distributed through local church workers.

Long-term aid (development aid)

CAFOD helps people to help themselves. There is a saying that if you give a man a fish, he can feed himself for a day, but if you give him a fishing rod then you feed him for a lifetime. Long-term development means bringing about long-term changes to communities in need, for example, improving access to drinking water and sanitation, education and tools, and providing money to start up local businesses such as farms. Long-term development is important because it allows people to support themselves and gives them a sense of their own dignity.

Case study

Uganda: children of war

In Northern Uganda, there have been many years of war, during which young people have been kidnapped. CAFOD helps those young people to return to everyday life.

One such girl was held in captivity for ten years and eleven months. She was taken captive by the North Ugandan rebel group, the 'Lord's Resistance Army' (LRA) when she was twelve years old. The girl returned from school one day to find her home surrounded. After being abducted, she lived in the bush with the soldiers in great danger. She had her first baby at thirteen years old.

This girl is one of 25,000 children that have been captured by the LRA since 1990. The soldiers want the children for use as child soldiers, sex slaves or to carry heavy equipment across great distances.

A CAFOD reception and rehabilitation centre cares for the children that return from captivity, helping them to find their families. They offer counselling to bring the children relief from the memories and fears of their traumatic lives. When this young girl managed to finally escape from the LRA, she was welcomed into the centre. Despite being staffed by only 12 social workers, the centre has managed to help over 3,000 children so far.

Activity

Identify as many different aspects of the work of CAFOD and Trócaire from these pages. With that information you could create a church flier or poster about the work of the charity, illustrating or creating symbols for the sorts of activities described. Think carefully about the audience you want to appeal to: adults, people of your age or younger children?

AQA *Examiner's tip*

There are three main areas of work for CAFOD and Trócaire. Make sure you can explain each aim clearly and give examples.

C   *Building wells is a type of development aid, providing safe water to communities in need*

Summary

You should now know and understand how CAFOD and Trócaire work for justice for the poor, raising money and awareness of their plight and providing short-term and development aid throughout the world.

6.7 Fairtrade and exploitation

■ Campaigning against economic injustice

Concern for the poor includes trying to prevent the causes of poverty. Christians have a responsibility to understand why people become poor and to do something about it. The commandment 'You shall not steal' includes taking a larger share of the world's wealth than is justified so Christians in wealthier countries are challenged to look at their own lives and ask if they are taking too much.

Beliefs and teachings

Neither thieves, nor the greedy…, nor robbers will inherit the kingdom of God.

1 Corinthians 6:10

> 66 *You are not making a gift of your possessions to the poor person, you are simply handing over to him what is his. For what has been given in common, for the use of all, you have taken for yourself. The world is given to all, and not only for the rich.* 99
>
> St Ambrose of Milan, 4th century

Exploitation of the poor

There are two views of doing good business:

1 Good business is business which makes money and that is that!
2 Good business means being fair and just in business and thinking about things other than just your own profit.

Many of the products we buy come from places we know little about. There are some stores with items that are very cheap indeed. Christians concerned with trade justice worry that the workers in some of the factories that make these products might be exploited. **Exploitation** might include child labour, excessive hours or a lack of safety clothing or equipment.

Exploitation of producers

Many of the goods we buy are made or grown in parts of the developing world. However, they are sold to us through larger companies. Little of the price we pay actually gets back to the farmers and producers in poorer countries.

Beliefs and teachings

The Catholic Church teaches that paying unjust salaries, something that is not enough to live on, is stealing.

Catechism 2409

An approach to business that makes the profit motive the only concern is immoral.

Catechism 2424

A business that turns people into things to be bought and sold is immoral.

Catechism 2455

Activity

1 St Ambrose seems to feel that the wealth that the rich have really belongs to someone else. Do you agree? Explain the reasons for your answer.

Key terms

Exploitation: when a person is used by another for the interests of the other at their expense.

Discussion activity ■■■

'Religion and business are two different things and they should stay out of each other's way.' Do you agree?

Activity

2 If you spend money on something made by someone else who was treated badly by their employer, suffered in their work place or was paid little or nothing for their work, does it matter? Give reasons for your view.

Fairer trading

The Fairtrade Foundation was established in 1992 by a number of charities. It campaigns that trade should be done justly without requiring anyone to lose their dignity, so that people are able to reach their full potential. It believes that the poor should get a fairer deal and that in business, one side shouldn't lose out.

Christian belief and action

The Roman Catholic Church teaches that one person should not exploit another. When there is this sort of injustice there are social and economic problems.

More and more people are concerned about buying products which are not fairly traded. Christians campaign alongside others for changes that will give producers and workers better rights and an opportunity to live dignified productive lives.

A   *Fairtrade products*

Research activity 🔍

Visit the Fairtrade website (www. fairtrade.org.uk) to find examples of the difference Fairtrade makes for the producers.

B   *We want trade justice! Trade Justice Movement supporters at the mass lobby of Parliament, June 2002*

Activities

3   Why does the Roman Catholic Church suggest that religion should be involved in business?

4   Give reasons why a Christian might agree or disagree with these statements. Then decide what you think and why.

a   'It is better that Christians pray for things to change for the poor, rather than take part in a demonstration.'

b   'Being like Jesus includes driving out trade injustice like Jesus did in the temple.'

Extension activity

Fairtrade gives practical advice of how to set up Fairtrade groups in the local community, such as in schools. Think about whether any of these suggestions work in your school. With your teacher's guidance you might like to put some of these suggestions into action.

- Set up a Fairtrade group to write a school policy. Adopt this policy and develop a plan to involve pupils in Fairtrade activities.

- Help the school to learn about Fairtrade issues in different subjects (for example, Business Studies, Geography, Drama).

- Encourage the school to promote Fairtrade activities in displays and newsletters.

Summary

You should now know that the Church teaches that business should be just and that one way of helping this is through Fairtrade, a movement which seeks to make international business fairer for the producers.

AQA   Examiner's tip

Make sure you understand how Fairtrade differs from charity.

6.8   War and peace: introduction

What is war?

War is a large-scale violent conflict. In human history these conflicts take place between tribes, city-states, nations and empires. There have been over 250 wars since the Second World War. Many of these wars were civil, internal disputes between different groups within a country.

What causes war?

There are many different theories about the causes of war and they come from quite different perspectives. Here is a selection:

- Violence is part of human nature but is usually suppressed. In times of stress, war is a way of releasing this violence.
- Wars are caused by expanding populations and scarce natural resources.
- Wars are caused when societies have too many young people aged 16–30, as young men are the primary killers of others.
- War is caused by economic growth and the pursuit of new areas of economic control, for example, seeking oil or gold.
- Conflicts arise when a country or an individual has a desire for power?
- Religious belief can sometimes contribute to conflicts.

What are the effects of war?

War affects individuals and communities: soldiers, civilians, the economy, society and the environment. Here are some examples of these effects:

- Wars in the twentieth century took the lives of a billion soldiers and civilian people.
- Hundreds of millions of injuries are sustained during war and many people die long after the war has finished – people are still dying of the effects of the atomic bombs dropped on Hiroshima and Nagasaki in Japan in the Second World War.
- Civilians suffer greatly in modern warfare – over half of the casualties of the Second World War were civilians.
- Damage to the economy is brought about by the loss of workers (killed or injured) and the destruction of infrastructure (roads, railways and industry).
- Wars can lead to long-lasting psychological damage on individuals and groups and cause enormous damage to social order when they occur within communities.
- Huge numbers of people are displaced by war, forcing them to abandon their homes and in some cases find shelter in other countries.

> **Objectives**
>
> Know and understand what war is and some of the causes of war.
>
> Suggest different short- and long-term effects of war on individuals and communities.
>
> Apply Christian teachings about respect for human life to war.

> **Discussion activity**
>
> In some parts of the world, people are able to live peacefully side by side, while elsewhere there is war and conflict. Why do you think this is?

> 66 War is the most barbarous and least effective way of resolving conflicts. 99
>
> Pope John Paul II, 1982 World Day of Peace Message

> **Beliefs and teachings**
>
> Because of the evils and injustices that all war brings with it, we must do everything reasonably possible to avoid it.
>
> *Catechism* 2327

> **Activities**
>
> 1   Look at the images on page 129. Explain how each image may be connected to the effects of war listed on this page.
> 2   Consider some current and recent wars. What were their causes?

A *During the Vietnam War the explosive napalm was used by the Americans, causing injury to civilians as well as fighters*

B *Troops carrying a comrade on a stretcher*

Christian beliefs about war

The Gospels have many messages of peace within them. Here are some examples:

- Disciples of Jesus should be peacemakers, not war makers. 'Blessed are the peacemakers, for they shall be called sons of God' (Matthew 5:9).

- Human life is in God's hands and is something no other human being should take. 'In [God's] hand is the life of every creature and the breath of all mankind' (Job 12:10).

- Human life requires peace to develop and war obstructs human development.

- Every human life, from the moment of conception until death, is sacred, created by God with a purpose and should not be destroyed ('Do not kill').

C *A war cemetery*

D *Psychological distress*

Beliefs and teachings

Respect for and development of human life require peace. Peace is not merely the absence of war, and it is not limited to maintaining a balance of powers between adversaries. Peace cannot be attained on earth without safeguarding the goods of persons, free communication among men, respect for the dignity of persons and peoples.

Catechism 2304

AQA Examiner's tip

There a number of different sorts of effects of war, on individuals, families and communities. Make sure you remember the different effects when answering exam questions.

Summary

You should now understand that war is a large-scale human conflict that can have many causes, economic, political, psychological and religious. The effects of war can be terrible. Christians are encouraged to work for peace and to respect human life.

Activities

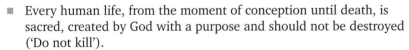

3   Relate the Christian beliefs about war to the other information on these pages. Then decide what sort of attitudes Christians might have towards war, giving clear reasons for your answer. What might this lead Christians to do in times of war?

4   What do you think the Church means when it says peace is not the absence of war?

6.9 Just War theory

Discussion activity 👥👥👥

1 Consider these views. What do you think and why?
a 'Some wars are right to fight, but others are not'
b 'When at war there are still some things you should not do'
c 'To win a war you must be prepared to do anything'
d 'War is always wrong'

Can war be justified?

War is often justified on political grounds: to defend your nation or to protect an ally who has been attacked. However for Christians to justify war seems difficult because:

- the Bible teaches that killing is wrong
- the Bible teaches respect for the sanctity of human life
- the Bible teaches that people should be peacemakers.

However, in Roman Catholic teaching there are circumstances when war in the form of self-defence is legitimate and justified and these are described as the Just War theory.

The Just War theory

St Augustine of Hippo (354–430 CE) thought that war could be justified in terms of self-defence and St Thomas Aquinas (1225–74 CE) outlined the beginnings of the **Just War** theory which explained when it might be just to fight a war and how that war should be fought. The Just War theory limits warfare and the effects of war so that it only occurs when absolutely necessary, for just reasons and is fought in a way which minimises the harm done.

When is it just to go to war?

The Table **A** shows the different aspects of the Just War theory.

Objectives

Know and understand the main points of the Just War theory.

Show how the theory determines whether or not a war is just.

Evaluate the arguments for and against war from Christian perspectives.

Key terms

Just War: a war that the Christian Church defines as acceptable: this must fit certain criteria. The idea developed by St Thomas Aquinas and the Roman Catholic Church.

Beliefs and teachings

All citizens and all governments are obliged to work for the avoidance of war. However, 'as long as the danger of war persists and there is no international authority with the necessary competence and power, governments cannot be denied the right of lawful self-defence, once all peace efforts have failed.'

Catechism 2308

A

Rule	Catholic teaching (quotations are from the Catechism 2309)
1. War must be a last resort.	'all other means of putting an end to it must have been shown to be impractical or ineffective'.
2. War must be for good, and against a serious threat of evil. The goal must be to restore peace, law and order.	'the damage inflicted by the aggressor on the nation or community of nations must be lasting, grave, and certain'. Trivial matters cannot justify war and neither can selfish motives.
3. There must be some chance of success.	There must be a reasonable chance of victory. A pointless war can never be a just war.
4. Weapons must be used proportionately – not excessively.	'the use of arms must not produce evils and disorders graver than the evil to be eliminated. The power of modem means of destruction weighs very heavily in evaluating this condition.' A war where the force used is excessive to the damage being done by the aggressor, can never be just.
5. Decision made by the lawful authority.	A war is not just if a private individual decides to raise an army and start a war. Only the proper government can make that decision.

If a war is just then the government must do what is necessary to fight it. Citizens should support the war and members of the armed forces should fight. However it is possible for a government to declare a war that is not just.

Problems with the Just War theory

Here are some questions which are not easy to answer from a Just War theory perspective:

- How can people be sure that war is absolutely necessary and that there are no other options?
- How can people be sure that victory is possible?
- Arguably, the main thing about going to war is making sure you win it by whatever means – the rule on proportionality means following certain rules in war which the other side might ignore, giving them an advantage.

B   *Who judges whether weapons are being used proportionately?*

- While war has traditionally been understood as a conflict between different powers, in the modern world there are many examples of conflict which do not fit that definition and so do not fit the rules of the Just War theory. Examples include civil wars (where one group of people fights another group of people in the same country), conflicts amongst minority groups who feel wronged, conflicts which intend to remove a dictator and government to replace it with a democracy.
- While it is clear that the armed forces might be a target in warfare, what about people who are working in arms factories, or those who grow food to feed the army, or those who heal injured soldiers so they can fight again?

Activities

1   Explain in your own words the conditions for fighting a just war.
2   Suggest some things which, in your opinion, should never be done in war?

Summary

You should now understand that Christians have many reasons to believe that war is wrong. However there is an argument from the idea of self-defence, formulated in the Just War theory, that wars may be just, under certain conditions.

AQA   *Examiner's tip*

Remember that the Just War theory is both about whether a war is justified and how it should be fought.

Discussion activity

1   Consider these two opinions. What do you think?
a   'Nuclear weapons are the greatest evil made by man, they are the opposite of the Creator God'.
b   'To protect yourself in the modern world you need a terrible last resort'.

Dropping the atom bomb

In 1945 America dropped two atomic bombs over Japan. Over 140,000 people were killed instantly. Many more were horrifically injured, and pregnant women gave birth to severely deformed babies. Many developed cancers as a direct result of the radiation they were exposed to. Today's nuclear weapons are far more powerful than those two bombs. The world's stockpiles of nuclear weapons have enough power to bomb the whole of the surface of the planet many times over.

The arms race and nuclear proliferation

Over the decades after the Second World War, many other countries created nuclear weapons, including Britain, the Soviet Union, France, China, Israel, South Africa, Pakistan, India and North Korea. During the 1960s and 1970s NATO powers and the Soviet Union accumulated stocks of nuclear weapons, each trying to keep pace with the other. The Catholic Church was deeply opposed to this arms race.

Nuclear war

The destruction caused by a nuclear bomb would be terrible. Anyone looking at the flash would be blinded. Everything within a few miles of the target would be incinerated within seconds. A hundred-mile-an-hour wind would flatten everything for miles around. Radioactive fallout would contaminate large areas, causing many survivors to die slow, lingering deaths.

The fear of **nuclear war** was so great in the 1970s and 1980s that many children suffered nightmares about the nuclear war. Many people became opposed to nuclear weapons.

Deterrence

There was a belief that as long as both sides had nuclear weapons no one would try to launch a nuclear war because the threat of what would happen would be a deterrence, that is it would discourage one side from attacking the other. This is known as the 'balance of terror' and some use it as an argument for keeping nuclear weapons and only destroying them if everyone agrees to do the same. Some believe that keeping nuclear weapons is a necessary evil.

The Roman Catholic Church considers the deterrence argument only to be acceptable as a step towards disarmament.

Objectives

Show some understanding of what impact a nuclear war would have.

Outline the dangers of the arms race and nuclear proliferation.

Show some understanding of why nuclear weapons could not be used in a just way.

Show some consideration of Christian arguments against the use and possession of nuclear weapons.

Key terms

Nuclear war: a war in which the participants use nuclear weapons.

Nuclear proliferation: the increase in the number of states that have the potential to use nuclear weapons.

Disarmament: when a country gets rid of its weapons.

Multilateral disarmament: the view that all countries should destry all their weapons at the same time.

Unilaterally disarm: when countries get rid of their weapons without waiting for others to do the same.

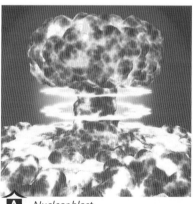

A   *Nuclear blast*

Nuclear proliferation

Although the threat of a global conflict has reduced since nuclear weapons were first created, these weapons are now in danger of spreading to more and more countries. The more countries that have nuclear weapons, the more likely it is that they will be used in the future. Terrorist organisations may one day have enough money to buy them or steal them. This **nuclear proliferation** makes the world a more dangerous place.

◼ Christian responses

Christian teaching opposes mass destructive power and its impact on civilian populations, communities, cities and societies. It is difficult to imagine a situation when a Just War could be fought with nuclear weapons because they could never be used in a proportionate way. However, some might argue that possession of the weapons prevents wars from happening.

Nuclear disarmament

Since the 1950s the Campaign for Nuclear Disarmament (CND) and others have worked for nuclear **disarmament**. Many Christians have been involved in this campaign and many people would like to see all nuclear weapons destroyed.

- In 1963 the Catholic Church called for **multilateral disarmament**. That means that all countries should destroy all their weapons. Some Christians have gone further and suggest that countries should **unilaterally disarm** (get rid of their own weapons and not worry about waiting for others to go first).
- Over time the Catholic Church has taken stronger and stronger positions on nuclear weapons. In the 1960s it declared that nuclear weapons and other weapons of mass destruction could not be justly used as an instrument of war.
- The Pope has recently again called for complete nuclear disarmament.

> 66 *Mankind must put an end to war before war puts an end to mankind.* 99
>
> John F. Kennedy

Beliefs and teachings

Every act of war directed to the indiscriminate destruction of whole cities or vast areas with their inhabitants is a crime against God and man.

Catechism 2314

AQA *Examiner's tip*

Understanding the technical language in this section will help you understand the main arguments.

Discussion activities

2 Britain's nuclear weapons systems are ageing and the government has decided to replace them with more nuclear weapons. The government feels there is a need to continue to have a nuclear defence. In groups, organise a debate on whether the government's decision was right. You may use Christian and non-religious reasons.

Activities

1 Why is nuclear proliferation dangerous?
2 Outline arguments for and against a country keeping nuclear weapons.
3 Could nuclear weapons ever be used in a proportionate way?
4 Could possession of nuclear weapons be justified on Just War theory grounds?

Summary

You should now understand that a nuclear war could destroy life on earth. It is hard to see how the use of nuclear weapons could be justified in a Just War situation, although some have argued that they are a necessary evil as they prevent war.

6.11　Terrorism

Discussion activities

1. Can it ever be right to use violence and fear to reach a political objective?
2. Why do you think some people become radicalised and commit acts of terror?

What is terrorism?

Terrorism is the use of violence to create fear for some ideological or political goal and deliberately targets civilians. Acts of terror include causing explosions, beatings, executions and kidnapping for ransom or for political reasons.

What are the causes of terrorism?

There are many different causes of terrorism. Causes may include:

- a grievance, along with a sense of not having any political influence
- political, social and economic inequality
- economic problems and high unemployment
- religious extremism or conflict
- ethnic conflict.

Experts today suggest that each of these factors have a role to play although political grievances and poor economic conditions are key reasons. History is filled with examples of terrorism and it remains a problem today.

Terrorism after 9/11 and 7/7

Today terrorism is seen in the light of radical militant Islamist attacks, especially the 9/11 attacks on the World Trade Center and the 7/7 attacks on the London transport system. Militant Islamist groups tend to claim grievances against some countries to justify their actions, including the Israeli occupation of Palestine and the war in Iraq.

Recent years have also seen the rise of the suicide bomber – a dangerous threat which is difficult to prevent. Terrorism now has a global dimension, as many parts of the world are affected.

War on terror, clash of civilizations or fighting crime?

Some believe that as a result of these attacks, a war on terror must be waged throughout the world wherever this kind of terrorism grows. This includes the NATO invasion of Afghanistan, the American and British invasion of Iraq (which some argue is illegal and unjust), and other military and political activities throughout the world.

Some argue that this is not a war at all. They suggest that terrorists are criminals. The language of war suggests the fighters are soldiers but in fact they are criminals.

Objectives

Define terrorism and suggest examples of terrorist acts and causes of terrorism.

Explain different beliefs linked to terrorism.

Suggest why some Christians might support the idea of a war on Terror and also why other Christians believe the solutions to terrorism are education and political.

Key terms

Terrorism: when groups use violence, or the threat of violence, to achieve their aims, rather than using a democratic process.

The teachings of Islam

- The teachings of the Qu'ran, as understood by Muslim scholars and believers, does not and has never permitted the use of suicide bombers or the taking of innocent life. The Qu'ran upholds the sanctity and dignity of human life.

- The use of suicide bombers has divided militant Islamist groups themselves because it denies Muslim teaching.

- Muslims living in Christian or secular countries believe they must live by the laws of that land.

- Most of the victims of militant Islamist attacks are Muslim.

AQA　Examiner's tip

You do not need to learn the teachings of Islam on terrorism for the examination.

A   *A bomber killed 13 people on this London bus; in total, 52 people were murdered in four suicide attacks in 2005*

B   *Attack on the World Trade Center in 2001*

Case study

Terrorism: the threat to the community

Terrorism threatens a number of aspects of community life.

- Members of the Muslim communities in Western countries are fearful that others will treat them in the same way as they would treat radical militant Islamists, causing greater divisions in society.
- Governments worried about terrorism may restrict freedoms in an attempt to protect the public.
- The terrorists themselves spread fear as well as injury and death through their actions.

How should Christians respond to terrorism?

The Roman Catholic Church has very clear teaching against terrorism in all its forms. Terrorism:

- prevents reconciliation between different peoples
- causes new problems and tensions between different peoples
- leads to suffering and harm.

The Church also teaches that even when force is necessary against terrorism, it is essential to address the causes of terrorism and promote respect for every human being and the unity of humanity.

The current forms of terrorism and the response of a war on terror are threatening the diverse human global community.

> 66 *The fight against terrorism must be conducted also on the political and educational levels.* 99
>
> John Paul II, World Day of Peace 2004

Activities

1. What is terrorism?
2. What are the causes of terrorism?
3. Consider the arguments for a war on terror and the arguments for political and educational solutions to the problem. Suggest Christian reasons for each argument and then decide which you are most convinced by yourself.
4. Think of some examples of threats to present day society that are caused by terrorism.

Summary

You should now know that the Church teaches that terrorism is wrong and should be resisted but also that the causes of terrorism should be addressed.

6.12 Pacifism

Discussion activity

1   Consider these three views. What do you think about each one?
  a   'Pacifists are traitors. They should be loyal, and fight for the freedoms they and others enjoy.'
  b   'Being Christian is incompatible with being violent.'
  c   'Violence breeds violence.'

Christian pacifism

Pacifism is the belief that violent acts are wrong and that only peaceful, non-violence solutions to disagreement should ever be used. Biblical teachings suggest that peace is a better way forward.

These teachings have led some Christians to dedicate themselves against any act of violence, no matter what the justification. The Quakers (The Society of Friends, a Christian denomination) are an important example of this view.

> *We utterly deny all outward wars and strife, and fightings with outward weapons, for any end, or under any pretence whatever; this is our testimony to the whole world. The Spirit of Christ by which we are guided is not changeable, so as once to command us from a thing as evil, and again to move unto it; and we certainly know, and testify to the world, that the Spirit of Christ, which leads us into all truth, will never move us to fight and war against any man with outward weapons, neither for the kingdom of Christ, nor for the kingdoms of this world.*
>
> from the Quaker Peace Testimony

During the First and Second World Wars, Quakers and other pacifists supported people who refused to join the army because of their religious or ethical beliefs. They were often given dangerous tasks as an alternative. These included assignments to be stretcher-bearers, sent out onto the battlefields to bring in the dead, or driving ambulances during the London Blitz. They would drive the ambulances with their headlamps off (because of the blackout) towards the sights and sounds of the bombings and into the bombing areas to search for the injured.

Beliefs and teachings

Blessed are the peacemakers, for they will be called sons of God.

Matthew 5:9

Do not resist the evil person. If someone strikes you on the right cheek, turn to him the other also.

Matthew 5:39

Put your sword back in its place, Jesus said to him, for all who draw by the sword will die by the sword.

Matthew 26:52

Objectives

Know and understand what pacifism is.

Give reasons why some Christians become pacifists.

Give examples of Christian pacifist movements.

Key terms

Pacifism: the belief that it is unacceptable to take part in war and any other form of violence.

> *Darkness cannot drive out darkness; only light can do that. Hate cannot drive out hate; only love can do that.*
>
> Martin Luther King Jr

A   *Martin Luther King Jr (1929–1968)*

> *An eye for an eye only makes the whole world blind*
>
> Mahatma Gandhi

B   *Mahatma Gandhi (1869–1948)*

Catholic approaches to pacifism

The Roman Catholic Church does not express the pacifist views found among Quakers but it does support the rights of those who object to fighting on grounds of conscience.

Beliefs and teachings

Public authorities should make equitable provision for those who for reasons of conscience refuse to bear arms; these are nonetheless obliged to serve the human community in some other way.

Catechism 2311

There have been Catholic movements that have been pacifist, inspired by the life and teachings of Jesus and the teachings of the Church.

Case study

Dorothy Day

Dorothy Day was an American journalist and devout Catholic who founded the Catholic Worker movement in 1933, which struggled for non-violent social revolution, labour organisation, civil rights and peace. At a time of the Spanish civil war and growing militarism in Italy and Germany, she grounded her movement on Christ's ethic of love and the teaching of the Sermon on the Mount. As a Catholic she thought that war was a sin against love and life and argued that we should use the spiritual weapons of prayer and the sacraments to resist evil, rather than weapons. She proposed that people should resist conscription into the army, refuse to pay war taxation, and refuse to make arms. She promoted the idea of community which had no national boundaries. In 2000 Pope John Paul II declared her a servant of God. She has been proposed for sainthood.

C   *Dorothy Day*

Activities

1   Compare the Christian arguments for pacifism with those that are in favour of a just war (Look back to pages 130–31 to remind yourself about Just War theory). Choose the strongest three arguments from each point of view and decide which you find most convincing and why.

2   In what ways did Dorothy Day live out the Christian message? Make links between her actions and Christian teachings.

AQA   *Examiner's tip*

Some people are pacifist for Christian reasons while others have non-religious reasons for being pacifist. Make sure you know why some Christians are pacifist.

Summary

You should now understand that there are many Christian teachings which lead some Christians to become pacifists. However, most churches are not exclusively pacifist, including the Roman Catholic Church.

6

Christian responses to global issues – summary

For the examination you should now be able to:

- ✓ know and understand the Parable of the Sheep and the Goats
- ✓ explain the difference between rich and poor countries
- ✓ outline the causes and effects of poverty
- ✓ give reasons why Christians believe they must do something about the poor and suggest ways in which Christians respond
- ✓ explain the aims and work of CAFOD and Trócaire, and their impact on the Roman Catholic Community
- ✓ explain what is meant by Fairtrade and why Christians believe that trade should be fair and should not exploit workers
- ✓ explain the causes and effects of war and Christian beliefs about war including pacifism and the Just War theory
- ✓ explain Christian beliefs about nuclear war and nuclear proliferation
- ✓ explain Christian beliefs about terrorism and responses to it.

Sample answer

1 Write an answer to the following exam question.
   Outline the work of CAFOD or Trócaire.   (6 marks)
2 Read the following sample answer:

> CAFOD raises money to help poor people in poor countries. They provide emergency help to people suffering from things like famine. They send medical supplies, food and water. They also help people get better at helping themselves. For example they dig wells and build water pumps to bring clean drinking water to people.

3 With a partner, discuss the sample answer. Do you think that there are other things that the student could have included in the answer?

4 What mark would you give this answer out of 6? Look at the mark scheme in the Introduction on page 7 (AO1). What are the reasons for the mark you have given?

AQA Examination-style questions

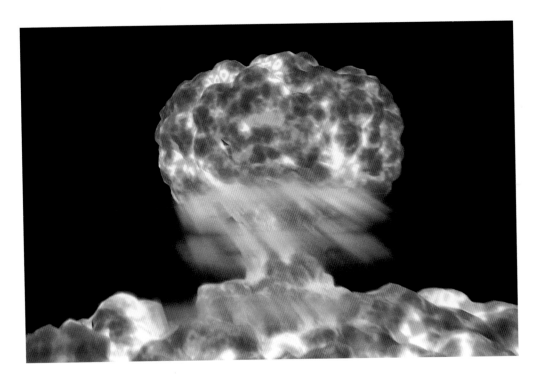

1 (a) What is mean by the word pacifism? *(2 marks)*

   (b) Explain why the Roman Catholic Church is in favour of the reduction of
        nuclear weapons. *(4 marks)*

   (c) Explain the causes of war. *(6 marks)*

   (d) 'A Christian should always be a pacifist'
        Do you agree? Give reasons for your answer, showing that you have thought
        about more than one point of view. *(6 marks)*

AQA
Examiner's tip Remember when you are asked if you agree with a statement, you must show what you
think and the reasons why other people might not agree with you. If your answer is
one-sided you will only achieve a maximum of 4 marks. If you make no religious comment
then you will achieve no more than 3 marks.

Glossary

A

Abortion: the deliberate termination (ending) of a pregnancy, usually before the foetus is twenty-four weeks old. Roman Catholics see this as wrong in all circumstances.

Absolution: the removal of the guilt that results from sin; the final part of the sacrament of reconciliation; forgiveness.

Adoption: the legal process where a person (child) is taken (adopted) into the family as a son or daughter.

Adultery: sex outside marriage where one or both of the couple are already married to someone else.

Annulment: when the Roman Catholic Church declares a marriage invalid. Various conditions must be met to prove this. For example, if one of the couple was unable to understand the demands of being married.

Anointing: being blessed with holy oil. This occurs during certain sacraments, e.g. the Anointing of the Sick.

Anointing of the Sick (Extreme Unction): a sacrament traditionally given to people who are dying, now also given to people who are ill or having an operation.

Apostles: the leaders of the Early Church. The word literally means 'sent out'.

Apostolic: religious communities which combine a life of prayer with a life working in the world, for example in education.

B

Beatitudes: Meaning 'blessed' or 'happy'. The Beatitudes is the beginning portion of the Sermon on the Mount. In it, Jesus describes the qualities of the inhabitants of the Kingdom of heaven and indicates how each is or will be blessed.

Bear false witness: to lie.

C

CAFOD: *Catholic Fund for Overseas Development* – a private charity established by the Bishops of England and Wales to bring aid to less economically developed countries.

Capital punishment: form of punishment in which a prisoner is put to death for crimes committed.

Celibacy: the obligation to abstain from sexual relationships; part of the vows taken by people entering religious life.

Charity: Christian action for those in need.

Chastity: making a vow not to take a wife, husband or partner and not to have sexual relations.

Chasuble/stole: these are the Eucharistic clothes of office – they show that the wearer is a priest.

Christian: someone who believes in Jesus Christ and follows the religion based on his teachings.

Christian Marriage: when a man and a woman come together and promise to live together in a lifelong, permanent and exclusive relationship.

Church: the holy people of God, also called the body of Christ, among whom Christ is present and active; Members of a particular Christian denomination/tradition; A building in which Christians worship.

Colour: relating to the colour of a person's skin/ethnicity. Often used as a reason for unfairly judging others and making uninformed opinions about them.

Commandment: a rule for living, given by God; One of the Ten Commandments.

Community service: a method of punishment. Forcing a person to undertake work for the community.

Conscience: a person's sense of right and wrong. For many Christians it is linked to God.

Confession: acknowledging and stating sins committed.

Consent: exchange of vows.

Contemplative: in the context of Christian Vocation, this applies to those who choose to live out their vocation in structured prayer, meditation and work, usually in enclosed religious orders.

Contraception: the artificial and chemical methods used to prevent pregnancy taking place.

Contrition: a genuine sense of being sorry for sins committed.

Covet: wish, long, or crave for something, especially the property of another person or someone.

Crime: not obeying a law established by a government.

D

Deacon/Diaconate: a minister who may lead some services such as baptism and marriage, reads the Gospel at Mass and participates in charity such as visiting the sick.

The death penalty: form of punishment in which a prisoner is put to death for crimes committed.

Death rites: ceremonies for believers in preparation for and after death.

Deterrence: to put people off committing crimes. One of the aims of punishment.

Dignity: the value of a human person.

Disability: when a person has a mental or physical condition that limits movement or activities.

Disarmament: when a country gets rid of its weapons.

Discrimination: to act against someone on the basis of sex, race, religion, etc. Discrimination is usually seen as wrong.

Divorce: legal ending of a marriage.

Donor: another person who donates sperm or ovum for a couple who are infertile.

E

Ethics: the moral principles that a person uses to guide and to judge their actions.

Euthanasia: inducing a painless death, with compassion, to ease suffering. From the Greek meaning 'Good Death'. Some Christians believe it is 'mercy killing' while others see it as taking life.

Exclusive: not divided or shared with others.

Exploitation: when a person is used by another for the interests of the other at their expense.

F

Fair trade: a method of trade in which the producer of the product receives a fair payment for his / her product, e.g. Fair trade bananas.

Fear: being nervous or uncomfortable with difference.

Fostering: the taking of a child from a different family into a family home and bringing them up with the rest of the new family.

Fruits of the Holy Spirit: signs of the Holy Spirit in Christian behaviour.

G

Gender: another word for a person's sex, i.e. male, female.

Gifts of the Holy Spirit: qualities from the Holy Spirit which will help a Christian to live a holy life.

H

Heaven: being with God after death.

Hell: being apart from God after death.

I

Imprisonment: a method of punishment. Taking away a person's freedom, usually in prison.

Infertility: an inability to conceive a child naturally.

In vitro fertilisation (IVF): a scientific method of making a woman pregnant, which does not involve sex. Conception occurs via sperm and egg being placed into a test tube.

J

Judgement: God deciding who should be saved on the basis of actions in this life.

just war: a war that the Christian Church defines as acceptable: this must fit certain criteria. The idea was developed by St Thomas Aquinas and the Roman Catholic Church.

K

Kingdom of God: wherever God is honoured as king and his authority accepted. Jesus taught about the Kingdom of God both on earth and in heaven. The rule of God.

L

Laity: members of the Church who are not in holy orders.

Lay Ministry: a role of service within the Church, such as a reader or a Eucharistic minister. All those who are not ordained are expected to serve God and others in their daily lives.

Laying on of hands: an ancient sign of the conferring of authority on someone.

Laying on of hands: an ancient sign from the Bible symbolising the Holy Spirit giving the person gifts.

Less Economically Developed (LED): poorer countries.

Life-giving: having the power to give life.

M

Marriage: a legal union between a man and a woman; The sacramental union between a man and woman in the Roman Catholic Church witnessed by a priest and the community.

Mercy: to be kind and forgiving.

Multilateral disarmament: when countries should destroy all their weapons at the same time.

N

Neighbour: a word which for Christians refers to anyone in need.

Nuclear war: a war in which the participants use nuclear weapons.

Nuclear proliferation: the increase in the number of states that have the potential to use nuclear weapons.

O

Obedience: obeying the superior (person in charge) of the religious order.

Ordination: the status of being ordained to a sacred office: a deacon, priest or bishop.

P

Pacifism: the belief that it is unacceptable to take part in war and any other form of violence.

Pastoral: comes from the word "shepherd" and is to describe the care that is given, for example by a priest to those in his parish.

Paten/chalice: these are symbolic of the priests duty as minister of the Eucharist which he then begins.

Peace: an absence of war and conflict.

Permanent: lasting or remaining without essential change.

Penance: an act, such as prayer, required of a person who has received God's forgiveness.

Poverty cycle: a cycle of decline.

Poverty: living simply and sharing talents, money, and material goods for the support of the community.

Priesthood: the roles and duties of a priest. Central to this is saying Mass.

Protection: to stop the criminal hurting anyone in society. An aim of punishment.

Punishment: that which is done to a person because they have broken a law.

Purgatory: the purification of sin from a person who has died so they can come close to God in Heaven.

R

Race: a group of people with the same ethnic background.

Racism: to have prejudices about and/or to discriminate against a group of people because of their skin colour or racial background.

Reconciliation: a sacrament in the Roman Catholic Church; When two people or groups of people who have disagreed or fought with each other make up.

Reformation: to change someone's behaviour for the better. An aim of punishment.

Religious discrimination: to act against someone on the basis of religion.

Religious life: dedicating your life to God, taking vows and living in a particular holy way.

Re-marriage: when people who have been married before marry again.

Resurrection: when Jesus rose from the dead after dying on the Cross. That other people may experience resurrection is one of the key beliefs of Christianity.

Retribution: to 'get your own back' on the criminal, based on the Old Testament teaching of 'an eye for an eye'. An aim of punishment.

Righteousness: following moral principles.

Rite: a set pattern of words and actions, for example those which are used in the celebration of the sacraments.

Roman Catholic: the tradition within the Christian Church which is led by the Pope. Seven sacraments are celebrated.

S

Sacramental: the importance of the sacraments, e.g. the use of holy water or the sign of the cross.

Sacraments: rites and rituals through which the believer receives a special gift of grace, e.g. baptism or the Eucharist. Roman Catholics believe that sacraments are 'outward signs' of 'inward grace'. Different Christian traditions celebrate different sacraments.

Samaritans: the Samaritans were mixed-race Jews. They regarded each other as enemies, so in Luke's parable of the Good Samaritan, the Jew had no obligation to help the injured Jew.

Sanctity of human life: the special value of every person's life. Christians believe that all human life sould be respected as a great gift from god.

Sermon on the Mount: a collection of Jesus Christ's religious and moral teachings recorded in Matthew's Gospel in the Bible, much of which Jesus Christ set out in a speech to his disciples from a hillside.

Sexual relationships outside marriage: sex between people who are not married to each other; this includes adultery, sex before marriage and casual sex.

Sin: behaviour which is against God's laws and wishes / against principles of morality. A thought or action which is wrong, we know is wrong and we freely choose.

Stole/chasuble: these are the Eucharistic clothes of office – they show that the wearer is a priest.

Surrogate mother: a woman who carries and gives birth to a child of another couple.

Symbol: an outward sign of something that is not perceived by the senses; it may be words, actions or objects and is important in the celebration of the sacraments.

T

Talents: qualities, attributes or abilities which in Christian belief are gifts from God and should be used in his service.

Terrorism: when groups use violence, or the threat of violence, to achieve their aims, rather than using a democratic process.

The Ten Commandments: a list of ten rules believed to have been given by Moses on Mount Sinai.

Trócaire: Irish word for mercy; Charity established by the Irish Bishops to help alleviate poverty in the developing world.

U

Unilaterally disarm: when countries get rid of their weapons without waiting for others to do the same.

Unmerciful: not showing forgiveness.

V

Viaticum: a Sacrament given to a person close to death to prepare for the next life.

Vocation: doing something for the love of it; A feeling that God is calling someone to a special ministry or way of serving others.

Vows: solemn promises that are made, usually with God and other people as witnesses.

W

World poverty: the idea that the majority of the world's population actually live in conditions of extreme need or hardship.

Index